Catch Me If You Can

Emelua Azuka

D1718739

Raider Publishing International

New York   London   Swansea

© 2008 Emelua Azuka

First Printing

ISBN: 1-934360-50-3
Published By Raider Publishing International
www.RaiderPublishing.com
New York   London   Swansea

Printed in the United States of America and the United Kingdom
By Lightning Source Ltd.

TABLE OF CONTENTS

Foreword
Rolling Stones
A Typical Star
Ground Floor
Race You Home
Walking with Fishes?
Total Recall
Growing Up
Growing Old
Did It Again
Quite Level
Beauty In The Beast
Measuring Beauty
Mirror, Mirror
A Number Of Questions
Go, Get A Life
Terra Firma
Dirty, Ragged Doll
Laughter Of The Gods
Now What?
Let Me Lie
Let Me Die
Tough Choice
Angazi
Live and Let Die
Catch Me If You Can
Knock Once, Barge In
Open Declaration

Black Coffee
Gay Sacred
Wicked!
Thank God, It's Friday
Told You So
C.V Says No
Fat Chance
The World In My Pocket
Count Me In
How High?
Foundations Once Destroyed
Tell Me No More
Count Me Out
Déjà vu
Definitely My Mess
Comrades' Haven
Postscript

FOREWORD

The first real echo I ever heard was simply the reverberation that come off the walls of an empty room, not that one could really call that an echo and, impressively for a six year old, I did not but I was fascinated enough to make the connection between that phenomenon and a real echo. If I had, instead, heard a replay of my voice, the words resonating back completely unadulterated and intact, I, most certainly, would have skipped back and forth, hurling every sentence I could devise from every angle and lapping up, with excitement, their repetition. It is, definitely a beautiful spectacle to see the wonder with which children look at the world, their minds experiencing for the first time, a dimension seen as separate and distinct from them along with the attendant nuisance, of course that their 'education' accords those around them. On the other hand, however, the gradual loss of the ability to wonder in adults is certainly a fate to bemoan; much more than a moan it might cost us, though, if we paid little attention to events around us and it is quite fair to say, I must admit, that we have not always done so.

I have always liked to think that I was the observant kind able to spot that the lad who had left the room three minutes before had returned wearing a pink brassiere; it definitely would not do to go through life asleep, to not 'stop and stare' every now and again. Of course, it would be ideal to be observant and questioning a level higher than a child, thoroughly ploughing down to the dirt core of the reasons why things work, as painstakingly and as clearly as possible. I had never really made any pledge to set myself to such a lifestyle or attitude, neither before a mirror nor in

5

those seconds just before dropping off to sleep. It was a habit that had wormed its way into my existence while a teenager mainly because, perhaps, I was never really adept at finding more involving ways of killing time or I simply had too much time on my hands. Either way, my thoughts always had the final say and even my mind was often helpless to the relentless lashing around of the ideas that had to be dissected, understood, defined and put to rest.

When I decided to put pen to paper to gush out this volume, I had no illusions that I would be rid of my 'demons' and I have not found any evidence as yet to the contrary. This book will not inform you on anything about how all we often seek to do as humans is to scientifically and methodically take reality apart, searching for conclusive answers and that we have grown tired of questioning wonder and demand solutions since I do too and have as well – as culpable as the next person in both regards. The only problem, however, is that our quest often ultimately proves to be in vain for the very nature of the world has always proved to be a mystery baffling us every step of the way, especially, just as we think that we have made some breakthrough in knowledge. It is a shame that our finite understanding is not fully equipped to grasp all of reality at once, perhaps, because our minds are not simply focused on the important thing - understanding the basic reason why we cannot. Over the years, I have tried to keep the sense of wonder that I had as a child and failed and, yes, often I find that is down to my sheer familiarity with nature. However, I have sometimes surprised myself by the path that my reflections take on the human experience of the world. The surprising bit, though, is that I have not sought to explain conclusively how things are or how they work – I would leave that to the natural sciences – but more, why they are. And, my quest has not really been to fully explain why, either, but to get some measure of understanding about the ifs, the whys, and the wherefores of human and natural phenomena.

This book is a collection of articles that demonstrates and elaborates on the trend of my reflections;

it is an open discussion on those questions that many might have asked, that many might have stumbled over and a few postulated theories on. However, it does not seek nor claim to give answers but only to demonstrate with a logical progression the path which my reflections on those issues have taken. It is also an attempt to find an echo out there in the minds of some who might have wondered on same questions or thought along same lines. And, even for those, who hold a radically different view, I can only hope that this work would offer some sort of standard and direction for a better understanding of what their positions mean to them.

In order to fully move along in harmony with this collection of essays, it is important not to see it as a treatise, a philosophical research or an academic expose. It is written in a light everyday tone and with a slight logical inflection. The articles of this book progressively lead from one to the other and begin from the beginning of our 'Time'. Gradually, 'Catch Me If You Can' ponders on the main themes that did arise and have remained on the journey of the Universe to full development.

E. Azuka

Catch Me If You Can

Emelua Azuka

ROLLING STONES

My very first stumble across the other side of Energy that does not openly showcase any of its finer qualities, that you may be aware of, did not expose me to any depth of familiarity with Light, much less, with how fast it travels. A lot of that association began, to my knowledge, with a man, who by the rather loud telltale signs on his quite familiar appearance, might be thought to have spent very little time in light. He did give us fantastical mathematical formulations of entities that we could not even fit in our imagination without tears. I will refrain, from sympathy, to boggle our minds with his attempts to show relationships between time and space via formulas or how he came by $E = Mc^2$.

I shall not dwell heavily on Einstein, however, but simply trace a rather famous quote of his - and this is what really interests me - that God does not throw dice. Given the fact that this statement came as a reply in a lively debate between the physicist and Bohr, debunking the idea of inherent probability in quantum phenomena, I find it quite easy to draw the conclusion that he must have been suggesting that if God did, then, it would have been nothing short of miraculous to generate the outcome that has become the Universe that we know. But then, again, since Einstein did not particularly adhere to a belief in a personal living deity or supernatural being, the notion 'God', in itself, does spell the miraculous if only to our finite mental capacity that strain to assimilate all that is hurled at us by the subtle intricacies of Nature.

For to arrive at that primal notion demands an explanation, which though seemingly deduced by bare faced Logic, cannot be grasped by it, unless, perhaps, there is a die involved in the equation after all – the little unknown factor, the principle of uncertainty by which the human is thoroughly befuddled and lured on to a never ending thirst to explore and to know but we shall return to this later.

And why should that be so strange when the utmost uncertainty in itself does exist, at least in paradoxical theory, that something might come to be out of nothing if all existence should point to one originating point and yet, no existential reality can be allowed to flout the seemingly unshakable law that nothing can come from nothing except, of course, (as some would hold) if it were 'God' or, as I might suspect, if Einstein were allowed some time on the problem.

And so this concept 'God' has come to represent the all encompassing point beyond understanding and the breaking point of Logic, at least, that of ordinary folks like us, so powerful that it has not a name except as a starting point to the sense humans might make out of their own existence. Thus, out of the incomprehensible seems to come our rationale and from the incoherent, our judgement. So maybe this smart guy got it wrong; maybe 'God' does throw dice and the result began in 'God' – confusing? Welcome to my world. As it happens, I suppose if there is this law in which the human mind can find no breach and with which our reason cannot argue, then, ipso facto, by that law is and should our Universe be made explicit to us. All reality within the reach of 'our' Universe should conform to this law or, by virtue of this same logic, should be classified un-real.

But 'our' reality cannot all possibly conform to this law (of motion and becoming) if we are to dig for the origin of all things. Therefore, does Bertrand Russell argue that if we would seek to provide a creator for our Universe, then we should do the same for 'God'. Or if we would claim that 'God' or the Prime Mover came to be out of nothing, we could, logically, claim the same for our Universe. Except, though, it would be argued in some quarters that the First

Mover, being the external force, lies outside our dimension and, thus, outside our laws.

Conveniently well put. However, if it is outside our dimension and laws and, thus, outside our reality, how can we confidently speak of that of which we have no evidence and with which we have no contact? Still troubling? We shall deal with this later on as well.

One thing is certain though; it does seem much safer to concede that our defined laws fail to apply to 'external' reality, leaving the question open ended, than to discount an arguably unimpeachable law and go on to entertain the possibility (as we are bravely doing already) that our beginnings would have stemmed from purely probable factors.

And that indeed does render our world totally contingent and, given that, furthermore, we have been judged by extensive research to be simply the ape that got lucky in the evolutionary process, there is found some base logic in the admission of the chance factor. And remember, fact is usually stranger than fiction.

However, the priceless [to me anyway] question is 'did the 'dice' have the same number on five sides?

A TYPICAL STAR

It does take little imagination to work out my chances at Craps if I could use my own such dice and I am not exactly referring to the very strong chance of getting caught. (Skip to the paragraph after the next to get the meaning of the following drivel) But, hypothetically considering the roll of such dice, the exemption of one side from total uniformity with the others does leave a real and significant enough probability factor. This would openly admit an element of uncertainty while offering a huge safety margin so potently alluring, the scheme is practically designed to succeed; where, ironically, design is the exact contrast to the very notion that the dice were meant to deliver. In realistic fairness, (and how even I would construct such dice) both numbers featuring on the dice would be extreme and opposite – in relation to reality, would be options such as: to be and not to be; vitalism and nihilism.

In effect, the question is; was there some direction inherent in all the chaotic chance events at the beginning of time?

So, by chance, (or not) there occurred the massive explosion that tore up into fragments, the hitherto closely grouped mass the Universe once was and by random chance (or not) arose the organisation of these broken bits into galaxies with each having, and formulated to have apportioned to each star in them, their satellites – parts of the aforementioned wreckage – and with the right conditions, generate organic life. Now, when I say 'or not', I am not referring to any purpose or direction but to the suggestion by science that when things are in the proper place and state, the ordinary processes of physics and chemistry take effect and take over, bringing about varied and visible results.

It does strike me as a startling form of design that obtains from total randomness yet, inherently, promising almost definitely to arrive at a masterpiece of a finish; (which we might have witnessed much more if we had not come along and spoiled it) a masterpiece replete with order and seeming purpose. Little wonder some have questioned the theory of randomness, equating such a view with another that a chimp given a typewriter might just, by chance, produce the works of Shakespeare.

Now, this might be totally laughable and it is not hard to see why, since the task for the chimp is to produce something specified and already in existence. It does not look like Chance can ever achieve such a feat, not even in the hands of intelligent beings; not even Intelligence can – it would have to copy to produce the original.

I have often seen, however, how from the results of absolute chaotic doodle sketched by the hand of a bored mind have appeared distinct and recognisable shapes more finely etched than the author ordinarily could. And an infinite number of chimps typing away for an infinite period of time might randomly bring up different words that could be all collated to produce works greater than Shakespeare's!

In evolution, it scarcely seems to have been about some intelligent patterning but about the fact that that which works, stays. Therefore, as Dawkins pointed out, atoms will always fall into a stable pattern in the presence of energy; no design there; that's just the way it is – end of story. So from chaos can, so often, appear order and from chance, design. However, it is a thought to muse over how long the mass had existed before the bang [far be it from me to attempt, now, the origin of the mass in the first place] and how long it took for the conditions to be perfect for the bang to happen. Was it bound to happen? Do we have, here, one of those situations where something need not be but given long enough, eventually, would – rather like the

15

theory (proven by me too) that tossing a coin often enough would produce an equal number of occurrences for both sides at some point. Of course, given long enough – eternity, no less – an infinite number of possibilities are achievable.

It does seem, therefore, that the very nature of the Universe in its apparent timelessness does offer the very tool with which Chance can strike at Design. And it does seem also that at some base level the principle that motion requires an exerting external force has been affronted. For staying within reach of our knowledge and intelligence, motion has arisen from within the agent and matter created from the, assembly, immaterial. And by randomness, could this be effected – a chance eventuality safely predictable among a very small number of possibilities, in fact, two: to be or not to be.

GROUND FLOOR

You see, the question, problem or possibilities given as 'to be or not to be' is quite understated in the exploration of its depth because, for instance, when I toss a coin, I realise I can only have two possibilities – head or tail. However, existence or non-existence is only one level and then, we have living existence and non-living existence, rational and non-rational existence. The question of 'to be or not to be' posed to a human would translate as 'to be conscious or non-conscious'; to a goat, as 'to be living or non-living; to a rock, as 'to be or not to be.'

Richard Dawkins in his book 'The Selfish Gene' takes us back to understand the basic steps our evolution took in answering this question at every known level. Of course, after the big bang – which dealt with the first level of existence - and in the presence of energy, organic substances in the primeval soup that scientists believe constituted the seas millions of years ago, formed large organic molecules. In time, claimed Dawkins, a remarkable molecule was formed which he called the 'replicator'; this molecule had the exceptional quality to make copies of itself. Dawkins made a small effort to explain that the 'birth' of this molecule was nothing remarkable in itself even though it was a rare chance occurrence – there was plenty of time enough for this improbable event to happen, for the replicator to be formed. Now, when I try to assimilate this teaching in scientific and realistic terms, I understand that substances, influenced by energy such as ultra-violet rays from the sun, banded together to form molecules for millennia, drifting about directionless in the soup until a particular association of molecules was formed that could harness and utilise the energy from the sun to its own end – it had its own direction. Now, it did not need to loosely and randomly form associations with other molecules with which it finds a stable configuration, depending entirely on luck; instead, it can make its own molecular copies by causing any attaching molecule to arrange itself in like sequence. This new quality of self-replication was remarkable as it was the first instance of a self-generated force which can be translated to mean 'life'. And no, Dawkins does not really care if we term this quality life or not, however, he does state that these replicators were the ancestors of life. But let's turn our attention to the influencing energy.

In the previous article, I mentioned how our reflections on the origin of the Universe might bring up the view that at some level, motion did arise from within the agent and matter created from the, assumably, immaterial. The 'assumably immaterial' – quite a posh sounding concept and if uttered in the right quarters, which would, generally in my experience, not be at home, could confer on one an air of learning.

Immateriality – I do wonder about that one. Elementary science does teach that matter is anything that has weight and occupies space and proceeded quickly to rule out of my [then] very young mind that even invisible substances like air could be material. Fair enough, but it becomes quite straightforward, then, to assume that non-matter should be the opposite of matter and devoid of its traits – anything that has no weight and does not occupy space.

In the world of Metaphysics, which for the most part studies 'hot air', this is a fairly familiar concept; Metaphysics deals with little else. Metaphysical Immateriality can be subject to neither observation nor experimentation because it falls outside the scope of our material reality; it can only be approached by some reason and some deduction peppered with a small helping of faith. This does confer a certain amount of exclusivity to non-material reality from the realm of science and to the field of

'Para-science?' For some time, this must have remained the norm with the physical sciences operating within only a certain limited area deemed to be material enough. Musings, though, of the questioning world did surface in different forms, in challenge of such an un-approachable metaphysical field, some of which were rounded and jocular riddles like; the 'how many angels can sit on a pin' question.

Parallel to the definition of Matter, however, is a definition of another scientific concept with which my rather amateurish mind, in fascination, does make an association. It is the explanation of a vector quantity as having magnitude and direction as opposed to a scalar quantity that has only magnitude. And, I do recall rather dimly that force is given as an example of a vector quantity since it has magnitude and always acts in a specific direction, as well as velocity and an electric field. On the other hand, mass, distance, speed and a charge are scalar quantities – all magnitude, no direction. These scalar quantities – I am getting a bit clever here - are all linked to or are a variation of the vector quantities mentioned; force with mass; speed with velocity; the field with the charge.

The one difference that stands out between both quantities, though, is the structure, predictability and definability that the vector has and the scalar lacks. On parallel, and in the world of scientific immateriality, the vector quantity would seem the material and scalar, the immaterial. However, the scalar quantity is actually the real factor and the vector only the measure or structure of the scalar. Thus, while speed is the main factor, velocity is the rate of its change in a given direction. This would actually make the scalar quantity the non-material matter and the vector the (non-matter) ^{2} - speaking in parallel and quite 'cleverly'. However, both are real properties essentially associated with each other and only by measurement and methodical precision do we prise one concept apart from the other.

One cannot say this much about angels, how happy they can be on a pin or the seeming nothingness out of which everything looks to have exploded into existence. Now, scientists have introduced to us a variation of a concept we have toyed with in the past, that is, the concept of pure energy as the absolute base of matter. Scientists now speak of zero point energy, the minimum amount of energy any quantum mechanical system, like the Universe [and/or/maybe what was before it] has and cannot be devoid of.

Now, energy is potential; potential for change; potential to do work. It is safe to say it is a physical – or scientific - non-material entity. It is also a scalar quantity and a form of 'non-material matter' if you remember my earlier adventure. But how real is it independent of all actual materiality?

RACE YOU HOME

My rather vivid imagination captures energy as some sort of real force capable of popping distinguishable matter into existence but then my imagination would rather like me in bed early enough. Because if prime energy does possess its own force as the denominator of actual matter, then perhaps, the question becomes; what feeds it, makes it real and from what does it originate?

Basic Logic should suggest – and this is not being clever - that nothing cannot be devoid of anything. If a system cannot be devoid of a factor, it is because the system owes it existence to the presence of the factor; take away the factor and the system collapses, that is of course, if the factor is not </= nothing, which would make the system non-existent. Energy, therefore, must first have been, and due to its presence, the systems of the Universe.

Apparently, from the observation of the effect of zero-point energy in a vacuum, it has been ascertained that: "a force, that has nothing to do with gravity or any charge, is exerted between objects". Surely then, this energy does prove itself actual enough, as non-material matter [an entity on its own] and also promises to have aided matter in defying the first principle of motion and 'becoming', that is, if we are to restrict our reasoning to our physical realm - material and immaterial. But then, when we consider that that this energy is not nothing, as demonstrated - immaterial or not – we are also drawn, at the very least, to attempt to account for its origin.

Energy, being a scalar quantity, should be potential to do work without, and not channelled towards any particular direction which should explain or by which we can surmise that it did have a random work distributive effect.

However, what might seem puzzling to many is the fact that in its randomness was achieved a principal set of conditions ideal for springing a Universe into place; a Universe that also demonstrated certain ideal conditions for sustaining a particular solar system, which in turn, too, met some definite conditions to generate life on one of its orbiting planets.

This is indeed significant when we consider that the conditions necessary to support and maintain the life – growing and evolving – that Earth boasts of are so finely tuned that the slightest imbalance in any of the pre-requisite requirements snaps us all out of existence, so have I heard. In addition, we might have to consider that the wonders of evolution in the adaptation of species and the intricate complex workings of the systems of organic bodies; the eco-balance of atmospheric gases in their cycles, plants and photosynthesis, the animal food chain and the organisation of consciousness – all weirdly arose from a random action.

My answer to this is that our real problem might lie in the fact that we very often try to trace our theories for the beginning of things from comfortable, easily acceptable and intellectually suggestible foregone conclusions. As gapingly unsound as the evolution theory might seem, it is not totally out of place to find that sometimes some sort of organisation is founded on chance actions.

There was also a rather intelligent line of reasoning I was really inclined to go down when I wrestled with my own theories for our origin. I would begin by taking you to the Ludo game. I can always accurately predict that if throw a six often enough, in fact four times, I would get all my counters out of the box; what may not be so predictable (and makes the game exciting) is how often the other player would throw a six and how my counters would fare against theirs on the home run. But I can also, with a little uncertainty, predict that if I throw a six significantly more times than my opponent, I would get all my counters home first and win the game.

There does seem evident from this little analogy a 'direct' predictability and an 'indirect' predictability; both are based on chance but the first is certain to happen and the other almost certain, only, depending on other chance factors. Still, given that Ludo is a game designed with certain laid down rules, it is easy to see why my 'direct' prediction cannot be wrong – because the game has been programmed to follow the path of my prediction; it obeys a law.

WALKING WITH THE FISHES?

There are a couple of direct predictive tendencies I can also identify about the evolutionary pattern of life on our planet and many more indirect tendencies. The basic structure of the path of evolution has been studied, or worked out, to have a certainty of direction. Given the conditions that Earth permits for the generation of life and for their development from uni-cellular to multi-cellular organisms, the path looks sure to be the same always; cell to organ to system; vegetative to sentient (instinctual) to rational (conscious).

What may vary is the method with which this path is trod or followed or, in simpler terms, exactly what animals end up being rational. I did see a documentary on how the intelligence of certain animals like dolphins are so highly developed, it represents a huge leap from the situation of many other non-human animals.

I think that knowing what we do now about the evolution of species, if we are put at the dawn of a new time on a new planet much like Earth to witness and live through a new process of evolution, we would not be able to predict with a great deal of certainty what species of animals would end up being rational, build cities and found civilizations or how they would look like. We can say, though, that given the same conditions that Earth had at the beginning, that this super species would highly likely live on land, have a large brain, be able to handle tools and generally have the form that we associate with primates. We can easily make this not totally certain but highly likely prediction because to dominate other species entirely and to use tools most effectively – both end products of a rational character – requires a physical frame most suited for a wide assortment of tasks, and the primate structure does foot the bill. But this is only an indirect prediction and dependent on any number of other factors that also depend on a variety of other factors none of which are sure to happen. Indeed, as has been suitably documented, the human could easily not have been. I suppose the same goes for every specie; one way or another, Nature would, most certainly, have found a way to channel its evolutionary track for intelligence and the attendant traits through some other species even if that meant that dolphins would walk on their tails, live on land, go on political rallies, organise circuses and juggle bananas – do not ask me how.

Back to direct predictions though. I am inclined to think as I have pointed out by the Ludo game analogy that these are so easy to predict because they follow a law, a program, a design; that with the development of one cell organisms to multi cell organisms come species of life with greater enhanced properties than the one preceding it. And so it carries on until we get to the greater and more complex development of the brain, which is for all species the control centre of what they are; and a complex enough and highly developed brain would at some point be capable of thought.

Laws are, generally [so I dared to say] universal, eternal, a program and set, which brings us around in a circle to, in addition to the drag about the origin of energy, the origin of any universal laws. More to the point though, was there some sort of law or set program that in the random chaos that definitely characterised the big bang and thus, the beginning of the Universe, there was bound to be struck, those very fine conditions suitable for our existence and without which the chance of that happening would be the same for throwing a knife at an unknown market crowd and expecting to pin the Caliph's daughter?

Well, all of this is one way of looking at it.

TOTAL RECALL

The problem and allure with any kind of thinking in the very tempting direction that I outlined in the last two articles is that it subtly promises us some sort of intention in our being and, therefore, purpose in our existence, that is – destined beforehand. It seems to me that all the elaboration on universal laws and how they are set and are a program and so on does not hold when we step away from seeing things that are, as a sign of things unseen that 'must have been'. If the pre-requisite conditions for life on our planet are so finely balanced, that is the more reason to understand that we so easily could not have been. Indeed the evolution of the universe won a major jackpot in striking the right conditions from which we have sprung and there was plenty of time enough for any such rare possibility to become realised.

No, indeed, I do not have an answer for the origin of energy, which is not nothing but seeing that I have to attend to this question whatever path my theory takes, I would, first, lay my cards on the table. The fascinating thing for me is that if we go far back enough, we should, logically, come to a point when there was nothing, perhaps, absolutely.

Now, I cannot subscribe to a Universe that came from nothing because that is ridiculous nor can I subscribe to a creating God because, among other things – some of which I shall deal with later, it is more difficult to create God (and we have to) than to create the Universe.

So I turn to Nothingness as the base and foundation of all reality – visible and invisible, material and immaterial – where Nothingness is not nothing but simply the absence of reality and the ever present potential for becoming. Well, this is my theory.

This is energy – perhaps at a level more base than even the zero-point energy of scientists, as pure potential and a negative reality that could never not have been. Does this totally wipe out all claims to and for supernatural reality? It sure does look like it because while we have science to test what we can lay hold of and logic to deduce that which we cannot, the supernatural has proved elusive to both well-springs of our knowledge, expressing itself as the subjective experience of individual minds.

I believe that all reality is knowable and within reach of the human experience which is why I am only prepared to go as far back as energy for the origin of things. Any claim to the contrary that some reality might not be knowable would be admitting knowledge of such unknown reality and its trait of 'unknowability'.

In essence, I did reach some conclusion that could be labelled as the five A's:

All reality is knowable

All precise reality is known, deductible and obvious

All general reality is elusive

All general unknown 'reality' is object of research

All precise unknown 'reality' is imagination

Until it is known or deductible and/or obvious, it cannot be categorically termed 'real'; of course, that is no claim that it is certainly unreal but a claim that it is the object of research as long as no precise definition of its attributes, traits or functions has been arrived at before the results of research show it to be so.

Therefore the only precisely defined reality we know should have been made explicit by research; any other is simply imagination. Every unknown reality under research such as the cure for some illness cannot have a precise enclosed definition and, thus remains a general reality – elusive. No general reality can be known; any known reality has to be precise. At least, that is what I can logically work out.

In any case, I will require another forum – indeed another book - to fully deal with this topic because the supernatural, be it a largely subjective field has a very strong impulse among humans. I would love to see just how much of it is objective.

Back to the point though, I look at it this way that the Universe and our world as we know it need not have been but has come about as the result of random physical scientific processes of change and development of substances powered by energy.

The German philosopher, Gottfried Leibniz expressed some faith, that we do have the best of all possible worlds. It has to be because it has been fashioned basically from drawing out the most functionality out of the associations of substances and organisms. Let us say we would like to think that this is the best of all possible worlds within reason.

Indeed, within reason, this world would be the best we could have as it has been made by us along with the random selection of species that have ultimately given it its present identity. Buried in this identity, though, has to be every stage of the growth process; the coming and going out of existence of beings, the extinction disasters, the physical re-structuring of the landscape, the adaptation of species and the appearance of homo-sapiens. And to think that our moment has come only in the last sixth part of the evolutionary timeline of the world, rather like, we are the Earth's adulthood. Yes, it does feel pleasantly good to hold that thought rather like we have held a few egocentric considerations in the past such as that of a geo-centric Universe; the presumptions of humans in their pride of place in Nature can so often run riot.

It did take some time coming, though - the development of the mind and our conscious ability to self-reflect, by which we stand separate from other animal species. Evolutionary research makes it clear that the gradual process, as it would be in any growth process, led from the appearance of certain primates to diversionary trends that led to the emergence of some other primate species from which humans descended. And there were the stages of homo-erectus and it sub-species that included homo-sapiens sapiens; wise man had come from a steady advance in physical look, make-up, activities and diet, all absolutely affected and in many cases, totally determined by environmental and other factors of climate, habitat and food.

The creatures of those phases prior to homo-sapiens sapiens were definitely also human, at least, in potential but naturally, we can only fully associate with the sapiens species because that was the stage we became aware and, therefore, as far back as we can recall.

GROWING UP

My earliest memories would be from my third year in life; that would vary among people but generally the birth of a mature memory strong enough to store and to recall events would fall at around the three to five year old mark. And that would be all we would be able to make of our lives; of course, Psychology might suggest that certain actions and experiences even from our conception can go so far as to have an effect on the people that we are, however, to all intents and purposes, we can only associate ourselves to the people we can only ever remember us to be.

Humans might be able to associate themselves more closely, if not only, with homo-sapiens sapiens but the traits and actions of the ancestral species would have left its mark; with every step on the rung of evolution, all characteristic traits are carried over in a more refined bundle with a few new traits added. After all, we are still hunters even if it is now with more refined weapons; we are herbivorous and carnivorous; we are still furry animals (if you disagree, go on a seaside holiday) and we are still instinctual.

But a lot has changed; we can work out why we do what we do and we can visualise our aims; we have language which is more than a set of signals but carry a lot of meaning in terms that do not give a call to action and we have non-action inspired humour carried in our language.

It would not have always been this way though. I may have been capable of some thought at age three or four but over the years, and with experience, my thought ability certainly has improved or should definitely have, signalling the different phases of childhood, teenage, adolescence and adulthood. With adulthood, I would not expect to see very many and rather drastic bodily changes - that is not counting the effects of the crushing, body numbing and debilitating schedule I might get up to in the gym - for some time but I can still expect some growth to keep happening. This growth can only, naturally, be in judgement and decision-making fed by the experiences gathered over years of trial and error and of mistakes and successes.

This becomes clearer if we look at our world as a sort of macro prototype of the processes of progress and maturation that we are used to witnessing in every individual species in Nature, and in ourselves. Every organic life is some sort of mini-cosm and in some way does display the attributes and traits of Nature. It is easy to forget that Nature is an actual living entity even though it is very much an object of concept. So, though, we cannot point out Nature, and please do not try to in public, we can actually feel her at work. If the patterns of growth and development in Nature have been shown to play out along the lines of from physical (body) to mental (consciousness), they have also been directly expressed in the same way in living things.

We start off the process of maturity from the womb and progress through to the first light of mental awakening; we learn to speak, assimilate and to think even more deeply; the body keeps growing until we get to adult maturity where there seems to be a stall in bodily growth but the mind keeps growing, learning, storing and experiencing. Even, when we become quite aware of our body's gradual progress unto old age and death, we, at the latter stages, are more focused on the mind and its function, giving rise to the widely accepted theory that the older, the [generally] wiser.

GROWING OLD

I have heard a few argue against the theory of evolution by the one claim that we should have seen some evolution happen to us by now. We should have evolved into something else, like the huge massive gaps that seem more and more evident between the physical appearances of certain people from what we would generally recognise as human, is not disheartening enough. Anyway, while I do not have a definite answer to the possibility of our physical frame becoming much more significantly different from what it is now, in the future, I do think we are experiencing that stall period in the adulthood of the world. I mean, it is quite easy to see that before the advent of consciousness, creatures were directed by the senses and by pure instinct; adaptation (by natural selection or otherwise) was crucial if a species was to survive and establish their presence in the world. So, various animals adapted to the differences in their situations that occurred over time from varied factors, chief of which would have been the climate and diet. But with consciousness and intelligence, there was and is, I hope, less need for compulsory adaptation neither does genetic variance offer as much hope for a gross survival advantage; humans could invent and use tools to limit and, where possible, eradicate their handicap. So, it might be a long call to expect drastic changes in our outlook anytime soon; or maybe, it is simply early days yet.

The huge changes we have seen, though, have been in the advancement of our intellect and our ability to self-reflect. Beginning with the necessary application of intelligence to inventions for our material needs, we have made great strides in the application of our reason to phenomena directly connected to our existence – issues that are hardly of a tangible reality like morality, society and structure, economics and religion. In time, we have made and experienced the disastrous mistakes of wrong judgement and, questioning, we seem to have made great progress towards a more balanced and more rational way of living.

I would imagine that the greater part of our evolution since we attained consciousness has been in the development of our intelligence, naturally seeking what would bring about a happy existence. It might have not been easy with the overall struggle to survive impeding progress at different steps of the way but immeasurably larger is the result of what such a heightening of our rationality has achieved. We can easily trace our progress from small groups to cities; from wars of expansion to the rise of kingdoms and, then, empires, the birth and spread of religions, the marriage of religion and politics, the resulting attendant tyranny of such union, the Reformation and Renaissance, the slave trade and it abolishment, Colonization and forced settlement, institutionalised racism and segregation, ideological Nationalism, the World Wars, the birth of the UN, the fall of empires, the spread of Democracy, the clamour for workers rights and so on.

We can trace the steady march of our intellect in pointing out flaws in systems and in behavioural patterns, in questioning the justice and efficacy of actions, in challenging and eliminating them and in being willing to make the ultimate sacrifice to see change happen. Now, we can look back at say fifty years ago and wonder at how people could have been so shallow as to have in policy a rule like Apartheid or how humans could have been so de-sensitised as to carry out the abominations of the Second World War. We may have that luxury now but there are a number of issues of our day that still need sorting for whatever reason or that are simply not being gone about in the best possible way. I fear my grandchildren would also ask how we could have been so shallow to allow some of what is going on at present to happen in the first place.

DID IT AGAIN

I really cannot say where this is all going to lead to and I mean the ongoing development of our ability to reason. After all, it is clear to me that with every step and at every stage of our history, there have always been new mistakes made and fresh lessons supposedly learnt. It is quite easy to find an analogy for this trend using our own individual experiences as a yardstick. Let me begin by saying that give or take a few un-orthodoxies, I am an everyday person, so I think a few people should be able to identify with me when I point out how often I have had to learn a lesson about a particular situation. There have been certain occasions when I have sworn never to go about an action a certain way again or have laid down rules about how to react to a situation if it ever arose. Alas, I have always found that I seldom have an opportunity to put my rules into practice because with each new situation comes a difference either in the manner it came about or in the people involved. Something is always different and I find myself making an excuse like 'that was different' and, eventually end up making even newer rules for the just experienced event, rules I know I may never have to invoke.

This also calls to mind a time when I was taking lessons in Zulu with a group of friends. One of them was and is still quite an impetuous character; he had a notebook with him and continuously pestered the tutor with questions about direct translations for English words. I could not help wondering – and I did ask him – if he planned to get a translation for every English word he knew and would possibly use in the near future, write all down, proceed to form every sentence he might ever make out of these words and, so, would have his Zulu all mapped out. It would seem a ridiculous and arduously difficult way to go about any language – he would have to be a monk of some sort to achieve that - when all anyone needed was the underlying formulas for any language grammar, and that is difficult enough.

I suppose it is always about formulas then, because, in my experience, the world, like our lives, is so diverse that it is replete with events and situations all varied and different as the people and places involved in them. So, we cannot hope not to make any more mistakes or to stop learning new lessons as a sign that we have achieved a full development of consciousness or intelligence.

This might seem to imply that all this theory about our intelligence developing cannot really be supported when all of our history might just simply be our encountering new situations and making new mistakes that we eventually learn from. I concede that as an interesting point to consider, however, my conviction that our ability to identify errors is more than just learning from mistakes stem from the fact that, in many cases, there had not been any unfortunate consequences for our 'wrong' acts (at least not for the perpetrators) but we still went ahead to overturn them. Take slavery, for example, or the struggle for women's vote; there were a few among the perpetrating caucus who started or joined in the struggle for a change when there was little they had to gain from it and a lot more to lose.

I can only imagine that this was because at some point, it must have seemed to them 'wrong' to carry on in the direction they were – where 'wrong' at this stage was not inspired by some impending disastrous consequence or punishment but only a deep and significant feeling of unease and discomfort which could not be ignored, explained away and certainly could not be silenced.

QUITE LEVEL

I believe that this phenomenon evidently denotes a deepening of consciousness and its maturation into being ever fully what it potentially can be. Now, I cannot claim to know the full potential of rationality but I think we are making steady progress towards finding out. I also think we are indeed finding out and making formulas for various situations and circumstances from which we have identified errors and/or learned lessons – formulas that may never be invoked in their pure form but that will definitely be called upon to inform our judgement on decisions to be taken on other new and likely different events. Some of these formulas, we have written down in charters and documented in pages but a lot of them are inscribed on the human 'spirit', which means that, not counting a few dissensions and hiccups, we would almost certainly have a rational formula for action when the occasion demands it that is not to be found in a book. I do not claim, either, that this is as black and white as I have just made it seem. We are almost certainly bound to make new mistakes in time and actually are, at present; I just think that there is a lot more documented in the human evolving psyche than can be held in print and the more we store in ourselves, the more our rationality and judgement deepens.

Maybe, though, we can lay some finger onto what consciousness could be developing into by looking at what consciousness characterises itself to be at present. It must have begun at the basic level of pure thought; being able to analyse and devise plans – for hunting, fashioning weapons, utilising game for necessary ends like food and clothing; learning from experiences – to discover and harness fire, sow and harvest crops, form groups and herd animals. I think the next and quite very significant phase of the development of consciousness was in the formation of language that would have begun as codes of signals as non-rational animals have.

The huge leap, therefore, would have been when human language began to carry meaning. I sometimes do wonder at what stage our ancestors, in language, could actually express and fully understand a statement like 'love is fantastic' and, worse, a phrase like 'quite level'. Sometimes, I do wonder how I came to understand those terms myself; really it is hard enough to learn to repeat 'a fat cat sat on a mat' and getting to recognise what the terms refer to. And that is the easy part because we can point out cats and mats, see the effect of 'fat' and demonstrate what 'sat' means but words like 'fantastic' or 'quite'?

We do not even think about these things; it seems most natural that we should know what they mean, not signify – because they signify nothing, not a noun and definitely not a verb. They are quite empty terms expressing conceptual reality that only a rational mind can fully apprehend.

Is it not a wonder then that we just pick up these terms in language and go on, over time, to grasp what they mean? Try explaining 'quite' to a child and you would have to involve words like 'very' and 'little' and some spectacle. And then, humour; once again, we do not often consider what a huge step it is that we can identify fun and humour in mere words and simply by communication so that we do not have to do a jig or make a demonstration to be funny, otherwise, a massive number of comedians today except, maybe, for Jimmy Carr would be out of a job. Our words carry in themselves enough meaning to evoke such a response.

All this seems to point to a phase when early humans must have come to realise that they could; doing or knowing is one thing but knowing that you can is QUITE a different matter altogether.

BEAUTY IN THE BEAST

It is certain to have been an overlooked phenomenon when humans could actually recognise that they knew or that they were really aware of themselves as thinking beings. It must have been overlooked because it all happened in a gradual process of evolution and people must have had bigger concerns then than dwelling on what new changes were being identified among their group. The first signs of the conscious ability of awareness must have been so subtle that early humans would easily have taken it for granted as something they were always capable of. I do not suppose they would remember a time when they were not aware with which to make comparisons because they simply were not aware at the time, just like we cannot remember a time when we were not fully conscious of our surroundings because we were babies or toddlers at the time.

Over time, though, we can safely say that this characteristic became the one factor that they became cognisant of; the one trait they must have felt separated them from the other forms of life around them; that gave them an advantage over other animals and empowered them to go out, hunt, kill, and subdue other creatures. Indeed, once they became mindful of the power of their knowledge, of their self knowledge and the power of their more developed minds, they would have gone on a discovery spree, trying to put this advantage to use, trying out new things, exploring new depths in their communication with one another and in the organisation of their little groups. Along with all this change would have, inevitably arisen, the whole question of how they would conduct themselves, what actions would be sanctioned as acceptable and what would not be – the morality question.

Teilhard de Chardin, speaking from a religio-scientific standpoint thinks that this is the real fall (what Catholics call original sin). Humans now have a real dilemma and, with the birth of the ability to raise questions on morality naturally came moral issues and, therefore, the whole concept of right and wrong, righteousness and evil, guilt and innocence. If I infer correctly from de Chardin's drift, then, the whole occasion of reasoning brings with it responsibility for choice and actions and therefore, the real possibility of guilt for wrong choices or 'sin'.

This might be one way of looking at it, however, I am more interested in the value early humans might have placed on what actions they would have considered wrong or evil. I cannot help but imagine that this would largely be based on the most natural rule of thumb we have available to us; act towards others as you would want others to act towards you. It would have been plain easy for those folks to rule out the killing or the deliberate injuring of another person and the stealing of another's possession as non-permissible actions. They would have viewed these actions to be obviously detrimental to the existence of any group or unit they could form, and without groups or communities, their operations for survival would, most predictably, be severely hampered. One thing I am convinced of, though, was that these codes of morality would have mattered only to the immediate group and within the group. Taken beyond the clan, everything would have been level; the killing of and stealing from another of a different and separate community would not have mattered. Morality was very much a useful tool; it was a means to an end and part of a framework for building their society.

MEASURING BEAUTY

Morality, for us today, though, is more than just as a tool or a safeguard from some unfortunate consequence. In fact, I believe if there were consequences as a direct punishment for our actions all the time, then, we would have little need for moral laws. All we would need to do is make up our minds to escape or face the consequent punishment and naturally, that would take care of guilt; apparently, that rule still operates for a good number of people which might explain the overcrowded state of a lot of prisons around the world today. More and more, it must have become clear to early humans that morality is not about the [direct] result of actions but about the value of actions themselves. So that at the end of the day, it bores down to the effect of our actions on the other and that another might have been hurt by our actions does evoke an unhappy feeling – guilt. And so, the moral question for humans must have taken a leap at one point to being more than a just a tool for survival.

Parallel (I do love this word) to the identification of inherent meaning in our language, so that our communication is more than a signal to action or a pointer to objects, is the realisation of the inherent value in morality. That at one point humans became aware of the fact that they were conscious beings and could carry meaning in their language, which for me is a hallmark of developing intelligence, also tells me that by that same process, they saw meaning in the moral question itself. At some point, humans must have discovered that not hurting another human went beyond the preservation of unity in their ranks, although that would be useful, but that it also went against something within them that kept them at peace. I would call that the guilt switch.

It takes a really maturing intelligence and consciousness to be aware of guilt - to be aware that an action can carry a consequence in itself; to from that action experience a funny out of place feeling; a feeling of shame, burden and unrest, a feeling that is more pronounced by the very state of being aware. Over a matter of time, the neighbouring clan would have ceased to become a legitimate object of destruction and plunder, except, of course, in war.

Yes, I am aware that it has been quite evident throughout history that humans have often taken leave of their judgement, of common sense and reason and have gone on ravaging destructive paths. However, I see these episodes as the exception and not the rule, besides, at the end of the day, we are still 'animals' and are to some extent controlled by impulses some of which would be greed and power.

And, of course, it is naturally expected that as rational beings, we would keep these impulses in check, firmly fettered from any wild manifestation but if we did that all the time successfully, then we would have to be perfect and ours would be a fairy tale and, I think, then, we would have no yardstick with which to measure or identify wrongdoing if we never had any actual experience of it. Not that this would be a huge deprivation – not having any experience of wrongdoing – however, I regard it as pure wishful thinking that beings who are capable of choosing their actions freely, would not at some point and again, choose that which is clearly, by their own judgement, wrong if only for the sake of curiosity.

Bottom-line, I do believe that we have made some progress in our ability to reason and that our intelligence has developed in leaps since we first became conscious and aware of our consciousness.

MIRROR, MIRROR

Indeed I believe that we are at that stage where our evolution is focused on the advance of our rational faculties and, considering the age of the Universe and Earth's evolution time, this has not been happening for long at all. We may yet still have some distance to go in the evolution of our consciousness; we may, indeed, be some way off the finished product whatever that might be. Our progression towards that end product or the idea of it, though, can only be enhanced, I believe, by our touch with other conscious beings, in communication and exchange. Indeed, we do take it for granted that a union with all of Nature is a healthy way of experiencing and going through life, however, I find that, taking this to another level, an even healthier way of attaining, maintaining and deepening rationality is by bouncing it off others with like qualities.

Is rational consciousness attainable or recognisable by an individual person alone? This is a question that I first encountered a few years back. At the time, it seemed that the alluring straightforward answer of 'yes' was in order, after all, did we not always have the potential for rationality in us and would we not have definitely achieved it, individually or collectively? But when I actually took time to study the question in depth, it became clear how difficult it would have been for any one human to become aware of themselves as thinking or analytic without another such like being with whom to compare 'ideas'. The potential for rationality can only lead to actual rationality given the right conditions and factors, one of which would be a community in and with which to affirm one's rational status. How would I possibly be able to tell that the thoughts I have and my ideas are of any real value if I could not find another who could put them to use. It might be a little difficult to grasp this fully because we are so used to the idea of being with others and being taken to be sane; it is very much like how I found it almost impossible to think of the concept of 'no gravity' as obtains in Space because I am so used to Earth's gravitational pull. However, take away the factor and the system collapses; take away the community and, well, you guess – or maybe this does not add up! Anyway, this might be why it is so easy for a person to go a little crazy if secluded from other people over some period of time.

I doubt that we are ever really sure of our own sanity by ourselves; we cannot be. We are only really as sane as the people around us and I hold that sanity is, therefore, relative; one's ordinary idea of sanity may not necessarily remain the same if they were removed to a drastically different and intense environment like a sanatorium, a prison or an insane reality TV show in that order. If I were kept away from other people over a considerable length of time, I suppose, I would, first, fall into a silent pensive mood and then to a thinking aloud mode, actively chat with myself, mumble incoherently, go wild-eyed, a little delirious, and given long enough, savage. Of course, all of this would take some time – plenty of time, even generations of lonely existences - indeed but these steps do signify a progressive backtrack away from a rational state.

The first two steps, I can identify as a means of reminding myself of what it is to be rational, what thoughts to have, what imagination to welcome and demonstrate, what words to say, what they mean, how they sound. It is a full reminder of the mode of existence I would ordinarily have with other people, that was acceptable by them and, therefore, confirmed to be 'normal'. I would naturally go through this phase so as not to forget how to behave with others when I am (in great hope) eventually re-united with them. However, given long enough, I would gradually forget these established rules of behaviour (sanity) and, there being no other person with whom I can confirm that my thoughts, words and actions are, for one, real and, two, that they are coherent, I would gradually, totally lose it or maybe not?

I daresay – very cautiously - that if we could have an individual live long enough over thousands of years alone, they would eventually revert to an existence that is totally devoid of consciousness and would absolutely function on instincts. Small wonder, then, that humans are gregarious beings; we have to be because it was by that action we attained the human state in the first place and that is the only way we can sustain it.

Although, frankly it is not such a big deal really, practically every living creature exists in community; it must be an instinctual drive and, really, there should be little wonder that we do as well.

A NUMBER OF QUESTIONS

Well, now that we have 'found' consciousness, what are we going to do with it? This is the pertinent question except it would not have been actually ever posed in as many words but in actions instead. Early humans must have been beside themselves in the excitement to throw up new challenges for their budding and very explorative minds. There was the world to discover and to understand and various questions to be asked about its origin. To put everything into perspective though, this 'question time' has spanned centuries and millennia. We can trace the very significant depth of human questioning to the time of the early Greek philosophers. Of course, I am aware that there had been civilizations and inventive scientists before that period and that humans had actually begun their exploration of various arts of culture, politics, simple machinery, warfare and law, to mention but a few, long before the Greek era. However, I (and a lot of the world) have been very much influenced by the questions, discoveries and theories posed by these influential Greek scholars.

I do think that we owe a lot to them since a lot of our modern knowledge is founded on the research that they carried out trying to understand our world – research in various areas especially philosophy, the physical sciences and mathematics. Several theories did arise in the questioning search that these people posed of the world; there were the theories that the underlying factor of the world was water, air, and fire and a number more I cannot possibly go into.

But I did find it of a particularly classy genius that one of them, Pythagoras, summed up the world in numbers. According to him, understanding the world and its functions lay in mathematics; everything is composed in ordered ratios and in a calculable pattern. He identified the mathematical ratios in musical notes and gave us the famous Pythagoras theorem. I suppose he does have a strong case when by studying the complex workings of Nature, it is easy to find a measure of ordered pattern; and it is easy to calculate and predict Order, hence, the whole notion that numbers lie underneath reality. I have a thing for numbers myself; it is so easy if we can work out almost accurately the relationships among qualities and things and the likelihood of events. Numbers are the only measure of organisation that we can play with and without it our world as we know it might descend into chaos.

However, can numbers always give us all the answers that we seek and help us uncover the 'secrets' of Nature? This has never really seemed highly likely, and at some point I am content just to stay with questions. Various mathematical calculations can only apply to some form of comprehensible, collected reality and collapses where this is not available which just might be, at least one of the reasons, why we have the notion of approximation in mathematics. I remember a certain tutor of mine asking a seemingly silly question; if $2 + 2 = 4$, what is 2 cups + 2 goats; no one, at the time, dared to venture an answer out loud for fear of getting caught up in some very deep silliness. But I figured that that was the stage where I would have to apply a common denominator for cups and goats or I cannot give an answer; the numbers only have an abstract value; cups and goats have a real value. We can only accurately calculate and employ numbers so much, and at some point, have to leave the rest to uncertainty or to stark cold reality. (further shown in the next article)

Much of our learning, though, has been inundated with numbers, calculation and Math. It represents for us the only way we can precisely study the confusing spectacle that our Universe can so often show itself to be and the sure way we might make some Order and some sense of our own where we find randomness and chaos.

GO, GET A LIFE

I did find Math intriguing while at school because after a while, I realised how, with it, we could decipher so much about phenomena with which we do not even have a direct physical connection. One such distinct scenario that stood out for me was the application of the mathematical formula determined for the measurement of speed given as distance divided by time in working out the depth of the ocean at a particular point. A sonar vibration is fired down to the seabed and the time it takes for the echo to reach the crew, recorded. With a given and known speed of sound, and the calculated time, they could work out the distance or depth. I really do not think that this is exclusive knowledge. Numbers, however, does throw up and present a certain picture of absurdity about the world and what reality really is. After all, in itself, numbers are a concept and are only a value that we attach to plurality. I do often wonder how our whole numerical system would be like if we only had eight fingers on both hands and eight toes. It is natural to assume [and work out] that early humans developed their numerical tally to correspond to the number of the human body parts most easily used for counting because it would have seemed the perfect example of a rounded and perfect number. So, we have a numerical system based on 10; even when I studied binary and hexadecimal systems, I always found myself working them out in relation to the quite familiar decimal system because they can be quite confusing. It just seems perfect that two tens are written as 20; if we operated on a hexadecimal system, would we not have to write two eights in a quite different and individual way? As it is now, we do not; when working out hexadecimals, we still employ notations derived for the decimal system and only make the mental calculation in hexadecimals; those systems are not fixed but dependent on the value and order that we have, ourselves, put into them, independent of numbers themselves - this is not really saying much, is it?

Anyway, mathematics does throw up the real notion of absurdity in reality or what we call reality. The basis of this absurdity lies in the infinity of numbers themselves, which, is directly related, I may venture, to the infinity of the Cosmos. About the greatest demonstrator of the problem that numbers make clear to us was a Greek scholar named Zeno. He presented certain paradoxes, a lot of which are directly related to mathematics and its employment in the evidence for motion (or non-motion as Zeno would have it) and reality. I have tried to take on some of Zeno's paradoxes myself and found the experience exciting. Perhaps, there have been found answers to lay his claims to rest, [that I do not yet know of] however, for centuries his questions puzzled mathematicians because these paradoxes zeroed in on the infinity in numbers.

One of them was called the Arrow. I will keep it simple; an arrow is fired and it moves a certain distance for a certain time. In an instant of that time, the arrow did move since it moved through the whole time, but that instant can be divided into halves infinitely, keeping the arrow unmoved as it cannot possibly cover an infinite number of half 'distances' to match the half-instant infinity. Or yet again, I walk from point A to B. To cover that distance, I have move through half that distance, and half of that and so on infinitely. Since, I cannot possibly move through infinity, I never actually arrive at B; simply put, I am actually unmoved.

There have been several 'solutions' given to these paradoxes, some so simple that it is so readily suggestive to people like; that human motion is about subtraction of length and not division. I have not been idle either; I have tried the theory that if we can admit an infinite number of halves for an instant of the arrow flight, we can do the same for the distance covered. The hitch still remained, though, that the arrow started from zero [along with time of flight] and so, cannot go back infinitely, making the whole thing quite absurd. So, none of these 'solutions', upon inspection, have dealt conclusively with the paradoxes. I do not, as yet, have an answer to Zeno's paradoxes; I would like to think I am still working on it but the more relevant significance of these debates is the immateriality of numbers and how the value we attach to them cannot possibly be totally correlative to our existential experience, not from where I stand anyway.

TERRA FIRMA

In the end, immateriality is infinite while we are finite; at some point we would have to loosen our grip on the immaterial, which may not be totally unconnected with materiality; after all, if numbers correspond to plurality in reality, its infinite and immaterial quality might point to same qualities in material reality. Nevertheless, standing on dry land, I can only say to Zeno that if at point B, there was a large tray laden with cheap liquor, not many people would be worried about his fears that they could never actually reach it.

I can also naturally suppose, however, that the one object of this academic search by these philosophers for the meaning and foundation of things is something that many human societies have at some period or another found a version of, and organised their lives around – a divinity.

It is so much easier and must have been so much easier for early humans to lay the responsibility of the creation of the world on some powerful and unseen being to whom they could also surrender the responsibility for their welfare. If the philosophers did not do this, it was because they wanted more than what seemed than a lazy easy way to solve a riddle; they would want some proof of the existence of some being or thing that could have been responsible for creation.

Ordinarily, though, it is easy to imagine that humans, not being able to recall beyond and before the sapiens species, would easily have credited a god or some external more powerful being directly with their coming into existence and over time, they would have felt a reciprocal responsibility to this being – to thank, to respect and worship, and since this being is so powerful, to ask favours of. One thing I can say about actions is that, like words, if they are repeated often enough, they tend to become believable, however, what may not have needed repetition in order to be believed, as far as early humans were concerned, was the direct yearning they must have felt for something more.

Now, this is where everything gets sort of circular; keep the next paragraph in mind as you read this bit. The mere trait of consciousness is an abstract quality in itself and it can only generate like abstract qualities. By rationality, humans can always ponder, investigate and question; the quest, therefore, for the origin of things or, a god, can also be seen as purely logically derived.

I believe in the sense of value with which the human is endowed; this value is absolute and draws from the fact that the human is a spiritual being, by which I mean, we can delve, in thought, into an abstract reality far removed from what is actual. I also believe that the human is more than just a complex pack of biological matter; we always long for something more; things that are infinite in value – love, peace, justice, beauty. Humans are, therefore, in themselves, a depth of mystery; this mystery searches for answers and will not be satisfied by something not complete, not absolute or not rounded.

The problem was that the Universe did prove to be a mystery as well to humans and so naturally, their hearts longed for something more, something not yet pin-pointed. However, what they found necessary to believe was that they had surely found a way to approach and harness the power of this great mysterious being even if it were rather unknown. They had to believe in the rituals and ceremonies they had established over time and in the methods of prayer and supplication and in the sacrifices and objects of sacrifice. They had to believe they had found a way to reach the spiritual with which they must have inexorably felt they had some association. This belief would have been the only source of hope they would have had to brave the life they had to live, the dangers they had to face from freaks of Nature, the diseases they had to endure and the rude, painful recognition of death. Yes, it had to be believed and, as I do hold, believing is a process of channelling energy into the mind on a particular theme and keeping that mental picture so in place that it does become one's own personal reality. Is it not a basic psychological truth that if the mind is attuned enough to a certain experience, it becomes real to the individual?

DIRTY, RAGGED DOLL

I really cannot claim to have a monopoly on the truth of what is real and unreal and what is true and false; I do not suppose anyone can nor that anyone should, and while I do believe that some objective truth is reachable in our experience, it does prove extremely difficult to get to it. Take the whole phenomenon of religion and worship that humans have nurtured for as far back as we can remember; it is very easy to cast, or to want to cast doubts about the usefulness or efficacy of the actions of the religious. In present times, there has been a huge rise in Scientism and, consequently, Atheism, or maybe the other way round; these would ordinarily discount religious practices as foolhardy. However, for the religious, the life they lead is their truth and remains a flag-post of substantial reality to them. The one problem is that we may not be able to ascertain that the relative 'reality' of peoples' religious experiences is confined, in their effects, to these people alone.

Not many of us might take the phenomena of occult practices, black or white magic, witchcraft and voodoo seriously but I think that the fact they have survived centuries does say that in some way they must have had some effect, real or imagined, on the lives of their adherents. I am particularly constrained to refrain from sweeping these practices aside as pure rubbish having grown up in Africa. First, I cannot because I cannot prove that they are 'rubbish'; I also cannot because such unfounded prejudice would only amount to brash ignorance and thirdly, I cannot because I have known people who have, or at least claimed to have - experienced the effects of this realm of belief and ritual in their lives.

Now, I will not be so bold as to say that by thorough analysis, I did identify that these experienced effects were definitely real and directly linked to the occult action they were alleged to have been. After all, there is so much Science can say about the state of the mind and various bodily anomalies that can so present themselves in the same fashion as the effects of some supernatural invocation. In the bestselling novel, The Exorcist, there was always a matching medical explanation proffered by Science for every state the 'possessed' girl got into, even when she demonstrated very baffling and seemingly un-human qualities, for which reason the use of exorcism was delayed.

Having said all this, I am powerless to explain some of the peculiar occurrences that have been directly and indirectly witnessed by people around me [as related by them —never seem to come my way!] especially cases where the 'victim' had no inkling of any such goings on behind their backs. You might indeed have your own stories to tell of rather unexplainable phenomena you have experienced – or have you? Nature is packed with mystery [or so it has seemed over and over again] so why should it be a wonder if we run into some of them. Atheists who strongly affirm the impossibility of anything beyond the human reality and the realm of science might so easily find themselves outnumbered, and might also find that they have to drum up 'scientific' explanations for lots and lots of quite baffling individual experiences.

Every religion has its own database of supernatural 'breakthroughs', which is probably why they existed in the first place – to reach and touch the mysterious. I do not think that I am in a position or equipped to question and test that – who is?; there are enough people in the world investigating this field anyway, and as I must have implied previously, there is only so much that I can observe and measure, leaving the rest to uncertainty. What I do question is the effect the whole exercise of religion, in belief, rules, practice and adherence might have or have had in the role of humans in the world and on our responsibility, if only presumed, as the guardians of Nature.

LAUGHTER OF THE GODS

Our religions definitely did have a profound and very significant [and, perhaps, still do] effect on our mode of existence for a very long time. Lives were fashioned by them; cultures grew and evolved around them; civilizations learned from them; kingdoms were sanctioned by them and our actions were dictated by them. I have found, in my reflections, that it is inherently a heavy burden for the rationally free human to have his acts and opinions frequently based on fixed 'unproven' and largely 'unanalysed' codes given by the religion of the people. It would not have been that humans had never in any way rebelled against the domination of religious values over their entire lives. The educated and the pondering ones in every age would have always questioned in some manner, the lengths to which they could go in being the sole decider of their actions. I can infer that this would have been the case because there is some evidence that religious principles had been questioned from as early as, at least, 400BC. Take the question that Socrates, a Greek philosopher posed, for example; he asked if something was right because the gods ordered it or if the gods ordered it because it was right.

There are massive implications that any answer to this question brings up – that right and wrong might be arbitrary values or that the gods were not the ultimate. I do not think though, that for many at the time, right and wrong were foremost on their minds when they tried to obey the will of the gods. It must have been more a matter of pleasing the gods. If they did not, then, there would be penalties; even the slightest abandonment of them by the gods could spell disaster. Nevertheless, I think that this would have only been the beginning of the huge incursion that their religion would have gradually made into dictating what actions of theirs were actually right or wrong. So, while in the beginning, they had to trust their intrinsic judgement to know what good and evil were, now, they no longer had to; the gods would supply that knowledge. The people would not even have been expected to trust the gods not to make a mistake; the gods could not – they were infallible.

I do not expect that a lot of us would bother too much about the almighty nature and power of the gods; what would thaw us (me, anyway) completely would be to think that not only were our rationally 'apparent' ideas of right and wrong discounted, values of right and wrong do actually depend on the whim of some being. And literature of some of the religions I have studied (and that you might have as well) do not show the principles of right and wrong by deities and divinities to be always consistent – not in manner, nature, or action, neither are they to our own ideas of these values.

I believe that this phenomenon actually marked the birth of a relative and first dark age – an age where learning was actually coloured, if not stifled, and blended into religious ideological tenets. As to be expected, religion would have slowly worked its way into the governing structure of the people and become the law. I find it quite logical since the surest and most effective way of conquering anyone is to get into their mindset and, by so doing, dictate their actions. This is the sole aim and power of brainwashing (the structure of religion as at that time); not many people can resist the immense pull of its force because they would be completely unaware that they were in that state in the first place.

NOW WHAT?

In a society where institutionalised ideology is entrenched by a process of organised brainwashing via religious codes, it is almost certain that anyone who resisted its pull would have been branded the enemy. This was simply why Socrates was put to death – for 'corrupting the young'. I would like to take you back at this stage to what I claimed a few articles ago that we are only as sane as the people around us.

Religion is a very sensitive issue, absolutely fed by things not seen or ordinarily experienced in everyday life. I really think that it does take a lot of commitment to give away one's natural rational doubts and accept certain religious teachings; it would have been seen, quite subconsciously, as a small step from losing a grip on reality – insanity. Expectedly, the society would have needed the back-up of everyone in it to assure itself that it was sane; they would need a uniformity of minds and hearts not only for their own satisfaction but to engender some spirit of nationalism, being of the same deep mental conviction. And at that time when wars were rife and kingdoms were rapidly expanding while empires were capitulating, it might have been a matter of survival to have and sustain a common and strong religion. This would have been the reason why, not only would the State have forbidden any teaching contrary to the religion, it would also have channelled its laws through the religion.

Before long, the issue of a marriage between religion and politics would have become quite common and this custom did persevere, as a lot of us would have learnt from history, for a very long time. Education would certainly have been squashed into a form chewable by the faith of the people; therefore, true and objective knowledge would have been quite unreachable. This is the main reason why I classify all the time before the reformation and renaissance as a relative dark age; true, there were huge advances in science and learning in all this time but how much more would there have been if people did not have to be very careful; how slowly the advance made must have progressed because of the steadfast and resolute adherence by the majority to tenets of the common faith even when they were shown to be implausible.

Yet again, it is testament to the development of our rational consciousness that humans became restless for objective truth: that they actually preserved the teachings of the few who had ventured to find truth and got killed for their trouble. It is testament to our growing ability to reason that at a certain time people felt that the power they had to choose their actions needed to be employed actively in their lives; that they ought to take their rightful place as the custodians of Nature; that they be the navigator of their course; that they should exist as the free beings that the very trait of free will gave them and that that freedom should permeate every aspect of their lives – in determining their moral norms, in pursuing research and in expressing their views.

I definitely believe that at this stage, and armed with a newly found freedom, there must have been frenzy among people to chase every, until then banned, study and open up every question. Evidently, at that time arose the most questioning minds that the world has ever had to deal with. There was a vast area to tread; rules to be redefined; policies to be reformed; societies to be restructured; economies to be redirected and moral laws to be debated.

LET ME LIE

I suppose that a brief summary of our morality would be that we would refrain from anything that would hurt or be a danger to another's wellbeing, as well as our own, I might add. Well, that is what it looks to be on the surface, however, about the most important aspect of our wellbeing is our life itself and any moral code would have at its centre issues on the preservation or better still, respect for life. This is where the whole conundrum does appear about different situations where circumstances might seem to permit the extinction of life - another's or ours. My brush with the debates, raging ones they have been and still are, has made me understand that these arguments are not in any way recent; a lot of them have been around for as long as early humans began to form communities.

I do not know for how long the issue of mercy killing or Euthanasia as it is better known has been on the table but it does not take much for my imagination to figure that some quite early human might have, with the consent of another, terminated the other's life if it seemed they were in grave pain, discomfort or danger that would lead almost inevitably to death. Euthanasia is still illegal in many countries primarily because it does seem to go in the face of all that is noble about living. And yes, we may ask exactly what this noble thing is and we would get the reply, life itself. I think, personally, that for some of the countries in which this act is considered illegal (and the ones I have been in) the primary motive for disallowing euthanasia is largely due to the influence of some overwhelming religious principle. Some religions, Christianity for one, would hold that suffering and pain is noble, wholesome, purifying and part of the human condition; that life is a gift from God and should be nurtured and protected; that God alone has the right to give and take life and that the extinction of human life is always sinful.

A number of people, however, would hold that the glory days of religion are over and that religious teaching should be duly kept to the side when debating matters that realistically affect people. I would also find it particularly difficult to buy into the idea that suffering and pain are noble and purifying because it is extremely difficult for me to really understand what those terms; 'noble' and 'wholesome' actually mean, neither would someone under morphine. How can we actually measure the effects of those terms in our lives in relation to the discomfort of a terminal condition; and if our lives are a gift from God – and now ours fully - why should he reserve the right to terminate it.

On the contrary, I would like to think that when it comes to the issue of the ownership of one's life, the individual should have greater say simply because they did not ask to be born in the first place. Why should anyone be expected, then, to carry the burden of a life that they never requested for, if it becomes unbearable? Euthanasia is particularly troublesome because it involves a second party on whom the blame for the death of the victim is so often heaped. A law against Euthanasia might also be in place out of a wariness of potential abuse by people doing away with someone they have deemed 'unwanted'. Well, I suppose there are always ways around that to ensure and adequately verify that someone's consent has indeed been obtained for the assisted suicide; because a law against Euthanasia is, in effect, a law against suicide, which, though is frowned at, is not actually a crime.

LET ME DIE

Suicide is about the most horrendous misfortune that can befall any person or rather the family and loved ones of the victim; it is a sore and painful subject, not least because there is always the feeling that the deed could have been prevented. This invariably and almost certainly leads to strong feelings of guilt among one or more of those left behind who may feel that their actions or in-actions might have in some way contributed to the death of the suicide victim.

I find suicide complicated to work out but one thing I do know is that the victim must have gone through periods of a hellish state of perhaps, depression, anxiety and/or anguish, or any many more states. No sane person contemplates or carries out suicide for the fun of it, except of course, if, bizarrely, it is some sort of coming of age ritual in the community, and, even then, it still would not be fun. More worrying, and perhaps, significant than the act itself are the reasons that lead to it. I would find it quite disturbing to think that a loved one of mine would have gone through so much stress and pain alone and unsupported so much so that they would eventually end up taking their own lives; indeed, it would tear out my insides. This is only a small fraction of what the families and friends of suicide victims go through.

Perhaps, the plight of suicide and its attendant pain helps to cast a shadow of grave seriousness on the various forms of self-harm; self-harm might be seen as a much milder manifestation of a suicidal temperament or intent; it is an act of rebellion against the self, just like suicide, only it does not necessarily lead to death. Again, more worrying than the act itself are the causes of it, which is why parents and families are heartbroken to find such issues in the lives of loved ones.

I think though, that a lot of times, suicide is more than just a rebellion against the self; it has so often been meant as a statement, a weapon against others to whom the victim's life is intricately linked and sometimes still, has been used to achieve a martyr's status or 'glorified' death.

If suicide is meant to be a statement, it does make a very strong statement indeed, which is why, except in very dismal cases where victims are at a very low platform on the will to carry on living, it does seem that a person with a network of people around them might just be a little more likely to take their own life than would a person with no-one to call family. I suppose that deep down, in a number of suicide cases; the whole issue is an intense and complex psychological 'game', evident not least in the factors surrounding the state of the victim. So that in the end, the taking of one's own life can sometimes be a means to an end in that it may serve as an escape, a statement, a confrontation, a payback or a victory. Take the case of Herr Goering, the Nazi, who 'cheated' his captors and the law by taking his own life. The blow of his death would not have arisen for purely selfless and sympathetic reasons; the pain was that of a loss and a defeat – that Goering did not face justice to the end.

At the end of the day, though, suicide is a terribly lonely act and one most excruciatingly painful, and I am not talking about physical pain. But the bigger blow always rests with the people left behind, which further goes to re-enforce the power of the community in a human's life and how in it, we are actually a whole unit.

64

TOUGH CHOICE

Suicide, however, in that it is not a crime, affirms the individual's right to make a decision on their life - to nurture it or to end it. The individual reserves this right completely; what they may not be able to control however, and which is always expected to be considered, is the effect of their suicidal action on the people close to them. The victims may not have asked to be born but neither did the folks who grew up around them; bonds of community and friendship are never planned or orchestrated and also without asking for it, we get 'saddled' with the responsibility of protecting the feelings of our community. This is the plain reason why the close unit around the victim cannot help but be devastated by the suicide; they have been drawn into a responsibility by the very fact of being born.

It does sound pretty heavy to me that by the very fact that I am human, I inherit several unshakable responsibilities and I cannot shirk them without denying my humanity or living against it – grave. However, by the same very nature of our existence, we could not exist happily without these responsibilities; perhaps, we could not exist at all. Thus we are bound to and are fulfilled in, and by our responsibility to nurture, protect and enhance the life of our environment, family, community and our world. A pain in any part of the grid will affect and be felt by all within the same network; but when there is a conflict of interest, it becomes difficult to know what pain to tackle; when there is a conflict in choices for individual welfares both attached to the family, it is hard to apportion priority. This kind of situation is depicted most clearly by an issue like abortion that is clearly a question of the mother's welfare against that of the unborn.

There have been several arguments put forward for and against abortion and some of these are not recent either; in fact abortion has been around for so long that Aristotle had something to say about it. For a long time, and maybe, even now, the focus of arguments was on how long before we can call the foetus, a baby and thus, judge if it is worthy to be spared. Aristotle suggested that abortion could be permitted up to the point where the foetus has sensation; others gave their own time suggestions but the main focus of the argument should be on the morality of the act itself. Some have said that the mother's welfare should be priority and that the mother does not have to go ahead with the pregnancy. Others have claimed that the child only has as much meaning given to it by the acceptance and recognition of the mother – quite controversial, if you ask me. One, rather bizarre claim, was that only that which has interests can have rights meaning that the foetus not being self conscious cannot have any interest in a continued existence and, therefore, does not have a right to it. This theory obviously opens the door to all forms of infanticide, which many would not find acceptable.

In an issue like abortion, I have always tried to keep a steady balance between the rights of the mother and that of the foetus (or child). And I have found that some people are quite cut up about the distinction between foetus and baby; frankly, I am a little as well, but more important to me is that the right of one should not unnecessarily outweigh that of the other.

ANGAZI[1]

I believe that sex is a responsible action and the involved parties have an inherent responsibility to the life that might result from it or to the prevention of pregnancy if they could not possibly bear the burden of a child. I also think, however, that mistakes do occur and, sadly, there is not so much we can do about that and a woman should not really be expected to carry and nurture a child she just is not ready for or able to cater for, especially, if she did take the necessary precautions or tried to prevent the pregnancy.

I would draw the line, therefore, at irresponsible acts of unprotected sexual encounters because one or both parties know they would always have the abortion option. I would call this wrong because by unprotected sex, the parties imply that they understand and accept responsibility for their actions, which could very well mean pregnancy. To go ahead, therefore, and have an abortion is a contradiction and would be inconsistent. There are several other situations surrounding the issue of conception and abortion that may give rise to debates on what is acceptable or not; personally, I do try to find some middle ground. I recognise the foetus is about every inch a human as anyone else, maybe not in the present, but definitely potentially; but I also recognise that the foetus can only achieve a full human state if positively accepted, recognised and welcomed by the immediate community which begins with the mother. This recognition would, in my opinion, begin with the openness of the sexual act to life, and, except in

---

[1] Angazi – Zulu for 'I do not understand'

67

really exceptional circumstances, cannot be morally withdrawn thereafter.

For instance, I do remember a friend of mine who suggested that she might consider having an abortion if she knew beforehand that the foetus or baby had downs syndrome. At first, it did sound plausible especially as she went on to claim that the child would only end up having a rather hard, uncomfortable and deprived life, likely to be rife with negative health conditions and ailments. I was, however, intent on the question: who for? All her reasons might just be true and might indeed come to pass but who is to say that the child would not welcome the chance to go through life, even with all that discomfort, if given the option. By the very act of openness to life in sex, the parents had accepted the possibility of a new baby and, therefore, accepted the child – a recognition that, I think, cannot be subsequently withdrawn without good reason.

Bearing in mind now that the child's opinion cannot be ascertained as to whether they would choose to be kept alive or aborted, after all, it is their welfare in question – supposedly - should not the only option be for life? In this way, we could not go wrong if, when in doubt, we opted for life. Moreover, there is always the deep question about whose welfare is really being protected; the child's or the parents; is it really the child being looked out for or are the parents actually concerned about the burden of raising an 'unusual' kid?

And finally, my biggest concern would be what is known as the 'slippery slope' argument; where does it all end? If we begin with the elimination of babies with downs syndrome, might we not move to babies [or foetuses] with one form of disability or another and then to malformed babies, ill babies, ugly babies, not so good looking babies and so on, until we would end up with 'designer' babies. At that stage, would we not have given over our rational responsibility to morality to an overwhelming selfish gratification that could absolutely disguise, if not wipe out, any trace of humanity in us? I really cannot say that I know.

LIVE AND LET DIE

A primary reason, evidently, for abortion to be so frowned upon – at least, when it has – must be that people generally believe that no one has a right to take another's life in whatever circumstance. Well, this view has forever remained debatable from assisted suicide to even the question of capital punishment where the State – the public – decides that one person should die.

The problem with a debate on capital punishment is that it is quite an emotive issue and the cold calculating logic that is definitely required to argue for it really does not become humans. This does not automatically, though, make capital punishment a bad thing, after all, where would we be without minds that can, when required, reason without getting bogged down with emotion and sentiment. I have a tendency to favour ruthless logic and, after once coming into close proximity with a violent crime that carries the death penalty and experiencing the terror of it, I put my weight behind capital punishment.

Some things have changed though; one view that I might have re-thought is in regard to the problem of miscarriages of justice that might see an innocent person executed. Ernest van den Haag claimed that such situations show flaws in the legal system and not in the nature of capital punishment itself and that life is absolutely riddled with actions of ours that cost human lives anyway. It may be comfortable to lay such an argument except when one thinks that those everyday actions like trucking and construction that cause accidents and deaths are not aimed at that but at production and except when one is on death row oneself.

Most things have remained the same, however, like my disagreement with the plain and curt argument that the State should not take life as an example to the people and that deliberate killing is wrong in every respect since, in themselves, these notions are as answerable as a contention that a Toyota Yaris symbolises freedom.

I believe, however, that an act of justified execution only dignifies the victim's right to a rational choice of either respecting other people's well-being and existence or destroying it. I also find implausible the argument that capital punishment dehumanises a society and puts into play a cycle of violence because that practically equates with the early twentieth century argument that humans refraining from meat would break the predatory cycle, curb aggression and stop wars.

Statistics have even been used to buttress this point about how countries with a capital punishment policy have higher murder rates. Well, the statistics did not reveal that a lot of other factors determine the criminal temperature of a society ranging from the family to the economy. A lot of countries today that favour the death penalty would crumble into chaos were they to abolish it without replacing that vacuum with measures to steadily tackle the other societal deficiencies that define their violent atmosphere. It is little wonder, then, that some parts of the US favour capital punishment when the country's constitution backs a ruling that people can own and carry firearms. In such a situation, if the country scraps the death penalty, some serious amendment must be made to the firearms law and to the various other anomalies in the country to avoid disaster.

Countries that run a federal system usually consequent upon being large, multi divided and riddled with socio-economic problems are more likely to employ capital punishment in the legal system as a means of, hopefully, controlling and deterring crime. I do not think that such a course of action can produce any beneficial results in any way since people will go to any lengths to get by if the State does not seem or is not being seen to help nor would they be deterred by violence or the fear of death if they have been brought up violent, unloved, disadvantaged, destitute and desperate. However, they would be deterred even less where the death penalty is not an option. Abolishing the death penalty, therefore, is actually a luxury that only a dedicated government can afford; it is simply a testament to the fact that the State might be taking a close interest in the lives and welfare of every individual citizen. So that, in the end, the death penalty which in itself, I do not find logically wrong, is a huge neon sign of an uncaring and irresponsible State that seeks the seemingly easiest route to solving a problem – that of violence.

CATCH ME IF YOU CAN

Standing away from all these arguments, however, I would favour abolishing the death penalty only because, in itself and due to its finality, it does not offer any opportunity to redress any mistakes in the execution of justice. If an innocent person gets sent to the hangman either erroneously or through a frame-up, there is no coming back from that. At first, though, I did try to get around the problem by working out very practicable guidelines in and for the employment of capital punishment. Such guidelines would only permit the execution of a person only if convicted on more than one count of murder thoroughly proven to have been deliberate and pre-meditated. Furthermore, on all counts, the accused must be proven guilty indubitably by hard, logical, clear, concise and corroborating evidence - such as a video recording of the crime - so that it is literally as clear as day to everyone that they were guilty. I also figured that this way, it would be awfully rare to send anyone to the gallows who did not so really deserve it; that someone would have to be terribly unlucky to be framed up on more than one separate occasion for cold blooded murder with hard un-debatable evidence. But since, there is no telling the depth of human prowess in plotting and hatching the impossible and the very real possibility of corruption in any human system however checked, I would opt for imprisonment.

It is quite easy for me to swap the death penalty for life imprisonment since I do not see it as any less mortifying being locked up for life and a life sentence does offer the chance for a reprieve should new vindicating evidence come to light. However, it has got to be a life term

– no less; that is the only true equivalent exchangeable with the death penalty and I am not talking about a couple of decades – it should carry on into the convicted person's twilight years. Perhaps, in effect, that is what prison should be all about – an institution for correction and rehabilitation that is not meant for just anyone. People have got to earn their place in prison; it should be hard to get in to and even harder to get out of. When we have inculcated in the public a healthy respect for prison, we might not have the recurrent problem in countries today of the overcrowded state of prisons.

The prison should be reserved for meting out more punishment than correction so that it is employed to keep those convicted of serious enough crimes and those that flout the conditions of their out of prison penal requirements from community service to parole. In all cases, prison should be meant to keep people in long enough to be feared, of course, proportionate to the offence and this threat should be made good. If the legal and penal system cannot ensure that their actions in the handling of criminals are anything more than patronising and laughable, we cannot expect that people would take crime seriously.

Perhaps, that is the one very slight advantage of a capital punishment system – showing the serious consequences of a wrong action. If, however, we are going to lose the death penalty, then, for our own sakes, we should not lose the severity that the arm of the law is, ideally, reputed to possess or we will be setting in motion the same disaster that does result from leaving a vacuum – that of the death penalty – unfilled.

KNOCK ONCE, BARGE IN

Going back to where I left off though, questions on the morality of abortion, in themselves, raise up several questions about the act of sex that directly lead to the issue of abortion. It is a rather difficult one, having a moral debate on sex. For a lot of religions, it is quite a cut and dried matter; sex should have no place in the human community outside of marriage and should be restricted between the parties involved in any union. However, this has not proved a practical rule for a lot of people to adhere to and not surprising since sex is in many ways the hub of the social aspect of the lives of animals, more so, humans.

This becomes even clearer especially when we consider the looseness with which it is quite frequently bandied. Well, it is also safe to say that a lot of people would take their sexual encounters seriously. And, then, we have to focus on what the term 'seriously' might entail; would that also cover the actions of people who market sex directly and physically? After all, it is a serious business, is it not – making ends meet?

Prostitution, often termed as the oldest profession, is often the object of not only debates but also endless government legislations. At heart, it represents the right of the individual to do with their bodies whatever they please; and, of more concern, once again, should be the reason why a person might take up prostitution, as it might be a starkly authentic measure of the economic reality of a people. Personally, I think that a lot of unnecessary attention is given to the act itself than to the causes of it; we may not be fully capable of rooting out prostitution from society [not like it is a disease] and if we tried, we may find that we are simply shooting at the moon since it is not reputed to be the oldest human profession for nothing. In fact, placing any kind of bar on prostitution would only lead to an underground, unchecked and uncontrolled form of it. Market forces are generally regulated by the well-known factors of demand inspiring supply but with prostitution, it is usually the other way round.

Various factors are known to drive people into the business, a lot of which are necessarily linked to a desperate need of money; to fund a lifestyle; to feed an addiction or, simply, to feed. It is a lot easier to raise cash via this means – the most natural business anyone can ever engage in - that requires little capital and promises no risk of investment; so that the more people there are willing to give, the more will gladly come to receive. Sadly, the State cannot, within the bounds of reason, place any kind of enforced limit or stop on demand, at risk of violating an individual's right, neither can it hope to even slow down demand by sermonising - the pleasures of the demand sector are too tempting for its members to be swayed.

The State can only work on, and with the supply whose crew would almost assuredly rather be in a different profession, their real condition going far deeper than the outward expression their occupation is. Basically, we have a responsibility to ensure that people are not forced into prostitution for economic or social reasons; when we have done that, we would have attended to the important issue.

It may be hard enough for a lot of people that someone would have to have sex with total strangers to make a living but infinitely vile is the idea that a person would be forced to have sex with a complete stranger in rape. I can only imagine that the crime of rape has also existed as far back as prostitution has, in some form or another – institutionalised or not. Various historic cults did employ some form of institutionalised rape in their rituals, identifying sex as a central act to their worship; it was rape because the girls had to participate sexually and not by choice. It certainly leaves little doubt that the priests of these cults and the male followers would have been fanatical about their faith for obvious reasons. For a long time, rape would not have been taken very seriously; it would have seemed almost the right of the male over the woman they have conquered, cornered, bought or married.

The Chinese sage Confucius is reputed (not verified) to have said that rape is physically impossible because 'girl with skirt up can run faster than boy with pants down' – rather thoughtful; the speed of the boy though, might be significantly altered depending on how far down the pants are, and would be if the boy were intent enough. Apparently, this theory did not seem to have stopped rape altogether in Confucius' day or he would not have had to speak about it in the first place.

In the end, though, institutionalised or not, rape must have had, to put it mildly, a less than comfortable effect on the victims and over time, would have gradually earned the distaste of people, not least, the family of the victims. With the advance of human society and the progressive empowerment of women, rape has come to be seen for what it really is – a vile violation of a person's privacy, wellbeing and right.

Perhaps, this would help us understand the power and effect that sex can have on an individual. By the law of alternatives [my private invention] if we cannot see the threat that willed sex might pose to a person's wellbeing, try unwilled sex. The disastrous effects and consequences of this, scaled down proportionately, might give us some idea of the threat that sex gone wrong, even when willed, can be.

OPEN DECLARATION

The discriminatory pattern that we have drawn from people's sexual preferences is something that is quite characteristic of the twentieth century. It is not that the kinds of sexual behaviours in question and that we are aware of today were not in existence in the past neither were they uncommon; they were just not broadcast before the public. The air around the subject of the sexual act itself was thick enough; to begin to hint at other variations of the sexual act would have been tantamount to disrupting the public peace. In those times, the world could only endure, uncomfortable as it may have been, an open declaration of heterosexual union; homosexuality and bi-sexuality were an aberration; in fact, it was not so long ago that I actually discovered that it was homosexuality referred to in the bible as the sin of Sodom or sodomy.

I do admire the resolution with which gay people have taken the long and painful fight, which in many places is still ongoing, to not only gain recognition in society but for other civil rights as well such as that of a legal union. There have been many attempts to explain the homosexual situation ranging from the theory that it is actually a psychological defect to the presumption that it is due to upbringing from a dysfunctional home. However, as it has been shown that homosexuality is not a new and strange phenomenon and that it has been just as much a part of the human experience as heterosexuality, we might ignore these theories.

I did have an opportunity to live in a house with a cat whose second litter was made up of male kittens. In time, the kittens grew and the mother cat disappeared leaving behind an older male cat – one of her first litter and some younger male cats of the second. The older male, cut off from mating partners, barred by the exit gates of the compound, did his business with some of the younger male cats. He did not choose to, being non-rational; it was just pure sexual instinct. Apparently, the sex was enough to satisfy him every time and we had no reason to fear there would be a new litter while the cat did not seem to mind. A tendency of this sort might be found among young people of same gender living together in one place, say, a boarding institution, especially if they are sexually active.

Unlike cats, however, the human, in an everyday situation, does choose their actions and their deciding to have sex with a particular gender must be for a reason good enough for more than plain consideration; I may not know why but then I am not supposed to, only to respect another's difference. Not many people would engage in sex that did not fully, or at least, hope to satisfy. Besides, it is easy to forget that the human body is beautiful – male and female; it is absolutely possible that some members of one gender can identify and fully appreciate exactly what the other gender finds attractive in them. To expect that every action of humans must remain set according to a well known and common pattern that some people would refer to as 'natural' reduces the human to a being driven solely by instincts and a being without ability to choose.

The human is a free being and besides the fact that that means that they can recognise right from wrong; it also means that they are not bound to instinctual drives; that their actions, I believe, carry within them, a certain level of unpredictability. I also think that this unpredictable element can be traced to the constant experiencing, processing, storing and learning function of the mind that brings about a frequent and regular variation in our perception of things, people, events and places.

BLACK COFFEE

I call to mind at this stage the huge amount of dust that homosexuality did raise in society from the time that gays began to demand a protection, through the law and in society, from discrimination. Their demands also had one aim, which was to bring about the legalisation of homosexual union. As to be expected, the outcry was more against than in favour especially as homosexuality was not really understood at the time and was not for a long time.

A big argument against it was that the act was unnatural; this was a reference to the claim that heterosexual union that leads to the birth and nurture of a family is the natural place of sex. In fact, Michael Levin claimed homosexuality was a misuse of bodily parts; that it was abnormal because the mechanics of sex demanded that the penis was used and meant for the vagina; I could not help wondering if, in the spirit of his terminologies, he would not, next, suggest ways of screwing and unscrewing the penis as you would the parts of a machine. Indeed, I found the simplicity of these claims quite hilarious, even if they might look upon first examination to make a lot of sense.

My problem would be the definition of what was natural. Considering, as we have looked at, that there is an element of randomness in Nature and in the origin of things, what is purely natural? Besides, upon analysis of the term 'natural', I cannot help recognising that it is really used as a substitution for the term 'usual'. Thus, people generally find that the patterns they are used to in Nature are 'natural'. Would this view, then, relegate to the dust of 'unnaturality' some of the past characteristics and actions of living creatures, that through evolution, have changed. I would, instead, call 'natural' those traits and actions that have either by evolution and adaptation or perception and choice, freely and necessarily appeared in the life of an organism, and not what pattern I usually find in their actions.

Having said this, I do not think it proper to claim homosexuality is unnatural simply because it is not so usual to our experience. Furthermore, plenty of weight was and, perhaps is, placed on the sexual act as being the route for procreation and family so much that it actually became a sort of dogma, that a sexual act was not right if it were not open to reproduction. This view would automatically keep out all forms of contraception and all other forms of sexual union.

I do not think that this theory reflects the practical situation of reality; people would hold sex to be, primarily, a pleasurable act of union in which they could celebrate love and affection; procreation would be a secondary function for the raising of offspring. Otherwise, if sexual encounters were always open to life or if people had sex only to procreate, then, either they would rarely have sex or be crushed by the sheer number of conceptions and, possibly, children they would have to deal with.

No, sex is not directed primarily at, nor is it mainly for procreation, which brings us to the nature of the act itself. For Levin to maintain that the penis is meant for the vagina brings up the question of the meaning of 'meant'. If anything, all we can judge from the nature of the penis, as a sexual organ, is that it is required and [sorely] needed for the act of penetration. This is the action by which the male gets his kicks; what may vary, and is not by any means defined, is the object of penetration (as we might, no doubt, be aware). By simple logical inference, the penis is not only meant for the vagina, except, and only if the couple were intent on conception.

GAY SACRED

Thankfully though, on many levels, the world has come to recognise that the rights of individuals to be individual in every aspect of living is paramount, so much so that the well laid out argument I tabled in the last article cannot really be of much use today. Fair enough. However, the complexity of the structure of the human society in the fundamental inescapable fact that the action of one always has or initiates the beginnings of a ripple effect on others have not really helped to lay the gay debate to rest.

Not too long ago, several countries, after making the bold and laudable move to legalise gay unions, have naturally made it illegal that homosexuals be discriminated against in any form or manner. Before long, strife and tensions arose between groups who, on the one hand felt they had to discriminate against homosexuals in some situations as a matter of faith or principle and the government who had to protect them – right from hoteliers who would not admit gay couples to the Catholic Church that would not allow gay adoptions from Catholic adoption agencies.

The debate that has been generated by the latter has not been, in any way, light-hearted since there seem to be grave implications for any course of action taken either way. Despite its past, (or should I say, because of it) the Catholic Church has remained ruthlessly efficient in carrying out social functions that do impact phenomenally on people, not least in the adoption sector where it has been remarkable in achieving results for even the hard to place children . Ruling against the Church, therefore, would deprive the State of this service; however, ruling otherwise would seem to go against a fundamental human principle which is to stand against discrimination. This tension has led to the closure of some Catholic adoption agencies most notably in Massachusetts in the USA and very recently, a threat of this same action was extended by the Catholic Church in the UK.

I listened for days to speeches made by Tony Blair and several politicians, as well as to other people's opinions on the matter. The main thrusts of arguments for either side have been: to let the Church get on with their job as the children's welfare is most important for pro-activists and not to give any group the right or avenue to discriminate against any person or group of persons for anti-activists. As I listened to more views especially stretched out ones that compared this situation with the conviction by faith that white South Africans had when they shut out the black people; or the conviction by principle of the Nazis against the Jews, I had a nagging feeling that some basic logical flaw – well, as I saw it - was being bandied, unnoticed, in these debates.

After some time to the problem, I have realised that what seemed to have been missed out is the fact that rights do belong to us all except in a situation involving two humans when there is or should be an elision of the right of one. I will spell this out comprehensively: the law (another of my invention) is simply that *in a situation **that might lead** to a relationship between two parties of equal rights, the rights of the subject cease to exist where the subject does not necessarily refer to the doer of the action but to the approaching agent.* The operative phrase in that sentence is emboldened – not a relationship but where one is being sought. To give concrete examples; a girl at a bar gets chatted up by a boy. The boy is the approaching agent and has no right to the girl; the girl, however, has a right to the boy if she judges him to be ideal for her. A job applicant has no right to the job applied for but the employer has a right to the employee if they are judged suitably qualified. Remember, this rule stands insofar as a relationship is being sought, so if the approaching agent loses interest, then this law does not hold.

In both examples, the right of the subject that does not cease at any point is to do the approaching; the decision on their suitability is solely the right of the receptor and can be coloured by their personal views, background, beliefs, culture and anything else. This decision is not something, however, that can or should be forced or legislated on by another. No person has a right to adopt a child – not like we have a right to buy an object; however, the child has a right to the most worthy adopting person or couple. We all have a right, though, to initiate the process of adoption but in the end, it is left to the agency to make a decision on our suitability to give the child the best upbringing, a decision that might be based on more than just visible evidence.

This decision is largely subjective depending largely on the principles under which the agency operates. Thus, a government agency might judge by State standards and a Catholic agency by Church standards but this judgement cannot be forced, pushed or penalised or we would be doing exactly what we are trying to prevent from happening to homosexuals – denying people or groups their rights to subjectivity.

Bottom-line is that Church has no right to stop gay couples from applying for adoption from Catholic agencies and the government cannot legislate upon what the Catholic agencies' final and subjective judgement will be. So homosexuals can and should be allowed to demonstrate their right to move for adoption from any agency whatsoever but if they do find out that for some reason, it is incredibly difficult to get a favourable ruling from a Catholic agency, then they should try elsewhere – that is what I would do.

This is not about the best interests of the child, gay couples, the Church or yet the State, I don't think; it is about getting logically as close to right as possible. And no, I am not Catholic; I am simply aware of what new pits such a legislation might be opening for society. This is based on pure logical reasoning – I very much hope.

WICKED!

And quite right too that every adoption agency wants to get it right in finding a home for their children because it is of paramount importance that the child is placed in as stable a home as possible. The biggest factor that might ensure stability in a home is a pair of adults in a loving relationship which is why about the most devastating aspect of broken non-unions is that the children of those non-unions are deprived of the loving attention and protection that only a full and secure family unit can provide; a lot of them end up in social or 'public' care.

Quite often, they would, in time, take out their 'frustration' on the society (the biggest victims of their assault being all forms of glass from windscreens to shop windows), which, probably, explains why there is the rising and prevalent incidence of yob culture, street gangs and violent crimes. It is important to note that I am not exactly talking about the effects of economic instability, poverty and lack as might be found in third world countries. I am referring to the actions of people, who have not got the right balance in their upbringing; who have not experienced the love and reciprocal responsibility in a full family and who, consequently, are not psychologically equipped to interact healthily with the larger society.

I have found that the huge fear of the institution of marriage might be related to the fear of responsibility in our post-modern thinking. If the whims and desires of people are to take precedence over everything else, then it would be a disaster for them to tie or restrain the possibility of full expression of their inclinations by going into any form of a binding contract. Unfortunately, the theory of the social contract by which Hobbes claimed that we are all in a contract with one another to obey certain rules and to be governed by certain laws requires a certain measure of responsibility on our part. If we shirked responsibility, then the contract would not hold, making our society an unstable place to live in. In simple terms and on a narrower note, this theory demonstrates that, at some point, we would all have to be responsible for someone or something else outside ourselves.

The unit of any society is the family and this is also the first post of any responsibility and, perhaps, of the greatest responsibility. I would expect, then, that to fully carry out our responsibilities in the family, we would need to be adequately committed. Unfortunately, it seems to me that the only kind of commitment big enough to capture the seriousness of this task and in which our role in the family can be suitably defined is marriage. As scary as it might be, and rightly so since it is a serious affair, it appears to be the only way we might really confer some respectability on the family that we belong to and are nurturing.

I, particularly, find that the case of a life-long unmarried relationship is rather lazy and also that - and maybe because - it does not expect or demand a lot from either party; if at any point, the responsibility they face becomes too tiresome, it is so easy and, perhaps so welcome, to walk away. Perhaps, that might be a good reason why the contract of marriage carries some harsh penalties for the couple should they go for a divorce; this way, it not only enforces some commitment from both of them, it also ensures that the parties give a thorough consideration to the thought of marriage before getting into it in the first place. Marriage has, definitely, not looked any less for the immature than at this present time, and it, certainly, is not being taken as child's play; however, by the same token it seems to be the one way that the couple can fully express their affection, respect and desire for the other.

I think many people would find it a little uncomfortable to raise kids outside of a marriage structure, not that they would be against pregnancy or child birth outside of wedlock but they would, at least for the security of the kids, prefer to have them grow inside a seriously committed relationship; this is why people actually take the time, and are encouraged indeed, to choose the partner with whom they might consider marriage. On the other hand, however, recognising the inevitability of human error, it would be far worse for the whole family if a couple stuck fast in a union that positively sapped the life out of them and that they both absolutely detested and loathed.

THANK GOD, IT'S FRIDAY

The upbringing of kids is an ever ongoing task and it certainly entails more than just teaching them about the world; it is also about building a relationship between them and parents. At some point, perhaps, we might cease to call it upbringing; this would generally be the stage where the kids would have attained not just adulthood, but also independence. However, the relationship and bonds that have been forged during the process of upbringing continue to play a major role in the dynamics of the parent-child co-existence.

Another relationship that parents have to ensure that the child gets into is that between the child and the wider society; this is by getting the child to learn about the structure of the society, its laws, language and customs. Usually, this education is offered in the home, among playmates and in the child's immediate surroundings but largely, it is offered by the institution of formal education. So, in effect, the child has to go to school.

I really did hate going to school all through my education (I hope I find company here); I would give anything for a holiday. It was worse in my first years at primary school; I had such an aversion to going to school that I literally worshipped weekends. And when, once, while in secondary school, a colleague of mine, out of frustration uttered a curse on the person or persons that 'invented' formal education, I could not disagree.

Yes, I could definitely understand the importance of education; every community and society has to impart the knowledge they have acquired to the young, but often, that knowledge was about the basics of survival and living and it was given informally without structure and without schedule. In fact every person, by the very fact that they are alive and in a community, gets some education. The problem I had seemed to be with the structure, intensity, length and variety that was formal education.

I have spent some time in actually pondering on the whole notion of going to school and getting a formal education especially in the light of the changing dynamics of the social and economic aspects of our world today. I was raised to understand that getting a formal education was central to any chance of success in life, and by success was meant being wealthy or, at least, being well off. I did not have to look far, though, to question that idea since my parents were well educated but remained regular people as far as earnings were concerned; they were not poor but they most certainly were not rich; they were, financially, nothing special. Later on, I became aware of a number of cases where people with very little education had gone on to become flamboyantly rich business moguls. These success stories actually sparked off among youths the craze to go into some business of one form or another after basic education, which would, generally, go only as far as secondary education level.

The commercialism that exploded in the world in the latter part of the twentieth century helped in entrenching this fashion as people could not identify the possible benefit of any education beyond the basics; college and university education became unnecessary; a few more would scrap all formal education if allowed. The teeming population of the world has driven the struggle for survival to an all time high and capitalist structures have fuelled the need to 'make it'. The ones who have 'made it' are publicly glorified by the media for all to see; following in their footsteps are the youth for whom the buzz is to engage in some form of lucrative enterprise; this also has to be sooner rather than later since there is more acclaim for the younger millionaire.

TOLD YOU SO

The last time I had the discussion of the importance of formal education with a friend, he told me of an encounter his uncle had with a bus conductor. The uncle, with a university education, held an office job of some sort and was on the bus, in his suit, on his way to work. The conductor, with likely only a secondary education (which is not so bad actually) brushed past him in his dirty greasy work clothes. The suit reared back involuntarily to avoid getting stained, to which the conductor sneered 'what has your education fetched you? I make more in a week than you do in a month.' The uncle simply replied, 'and look where it has got you.'

Although unlikely, it is actually not impossible that the conductor – poor chap - might have made some responsible investment with his money; the uncle was, however, referring to the likelihood that he had not. Einstein did say that 'education is what remains after we have forgotten everything learnt in school'; the structure, intensity and content of formal education certainly does leave its mark which may not be readily distinguishable but, doubtlessly, colours the perception and attitude of the educated. Of course, there are always different levels of formal education and for each level attained, there is an imprint left, an effect on the mind trained and educated that goes beyond the actual discipline studied.

In many countries, a marked distinction between the formally educated and the illiterate would be the skill of a particular language; say for non-English speaking countries, the mark of the educated would be a mastery of the English language. This would not, however, show a distinction between those with only a secondary education from those with a university education, at least not immediately. In countries, however, with a common language, this fails to be a distinction; but, in many instances, some distinction might be identified, the main one being a versatility displayed in judgement, knowledge, know-how, organisation and actual application.

This must be the main benefit of formal education, I think; yes, it is the avenue by which the world imparts knowledge to the young, knowledge that has been acquired over millennia of research and observation and knowledge that we cannot afford to lose. The basics of such knowledge would require a rigorous structured schedule over, at least, a third of a person's lifetime to acquire in school. Indeed, we might find that over time a lot of what we study at school would end up being, on the face of it, useless to us. What may not be evident, however, is that we have been given the most important skill of versatility; if we ever happen to be faced with a problem or a challenge, we would find, lurking somewhere in our knowledgebase, some skill with which to, at least, understand it. The uneducated, at whatever level, are limited in their versatility in inverse proportions to the amount of formal education received.

By formal education, not only does the world ensure that we can only move forward in our acquisition of knowledge, building on the knowledge that has been handed on, it also ensures that the skill with which to apply that knowledge has been passed on.

The wide distribution of disciplines and skills in formal education makes certain that the world always has a back-up option on skilled personnel in whatever field. The aim of formal education is to explosively develop the human to their full potential, which denotes real accomplishment and the true meaning of success. So, indeed, formal education is meant to make us successful, which is really a lot more valuable than merely being wealthy because if the world lost that factor, we would have to begin our journey of knowledge again from scratch and that would involve having to re-write the Principia Mathematica!

C.V SAYS NO

It is difficult to think of the world, in states and governments, not carrying out the important responsibility of bringing formal education to as many people as possible within their regions. Even with economic problems and activities disruptive to daily living rife in many countries, the importance of the education [formally] of children is still emphasized. It might be hard to imagine formal education being neglected with all the current legislations about the right of everyone to get an education and the enforced law that all children go to school. However, losing the benefits of formal education may come about in more subtle and gradual forms.

In my perception, the world is experiencing now, more than ever before, a gradual decay in the structural value placed on education. This decay has been, largely, due to the overwhelming and overriding influence of commercialism and its attendant drive to acquire wealth. Getting a formal education beyond the basic is not a totally welcome idea among many people; it becomes an aching concern, therefore, that if this view gets widespread enough and, with the results not likely to be immediately evident, who can tell what other levels of education might be neglected in time?

I have noticed that, at no other period in human history, have formal education been more 'dispensable' to the function of society. I have seen university graduates competing for same jobs as people without a college education, their skills and education not enough to give them access to the fields they have been precisely trained for. There is a very noticeable value placed on, and a growing need, for hands on experience; sadly the one who applies themselves practically to a particular field over a period of time is not likely to be the fully formally educated one. Education takes time and full education takes a lot of time; the world is, at present, in a huge rush to make money at an ever faster and crippling pace than ever before experienced. Entrepreneurs do not have any time for the 'pearls' of wisdom that the graduate might claim to possess; they would prefer the practical skill of the person on the street.

I read an article in a magazine some time ago that lamented the retrogression only vaguely evident, as far as education and learning was concerned; the article stressed that the world was approaching a new dark age (if not already in it) According to the piece, we have registered a huge drop in inventions and inventiveness for a very long period of time and more worrying is the fact that the level of our progress in discovering and ideas formation seems to have severely lapsed.

I have no way to tell the accuracy of this claim about the drop in inventions neither would I suppose that a majority of us would be unduly concerned about that. It does seem to me that the world is at present bursting with inventions that can cater to about every human need that we are aware of. Nevertheless, if there has been a drop in the inventive initiative or the explorative side of the world, then, that would raise a worry that goes beyond the mere number of inventions turned out. It would mean that learning and advancement in thought that should be a continually deepening thing has stifled. It would mean that human progress in knowledge is slowing or would slow down, if not stop altogether. More disconcertingly, it would spell the steady advance towards a time when we would generally lack the skills to apply the knowledge already acquired and stored, which like pulling on a thread, might be the first stage towards the complete unravelling of the structure that formal education has established so far in human history.

THE WORLD IN MY POCKET

My latter teenage years involved a period I still refer to as gloomy. It boasted nothing exciting or challenging to look forward to; it was that period where I was forcibly immersed into the world of adults, had to live by their rules and walk in their steps; it was the period where I recorded my highest ever use of the word 'bored'.

That was the period immediately preceding early adulthood and the years at university, which was for me everything that the gloomy period was not. All of sudden, it seemed that the world shone again; everything was bright and beautiful; there was never a shortage of things to do, challenges to see to, achievements to conquer and friends to hang about with. It was the period when I had the world in my pocket.

The most busy period in any life of any city is at the start of the University year when the city is bursting with young students who are not only raring to grasp every knowledge the University has to impart but also ready to change the city and to change the world. Students at that age are literally on top of the world; nothing is too big to achieve and no task is too daunting; friends abound and the number and variety of activities they get up to is endless. It is no wonder then that every university is inundated by the number of organisations, clubs, groups and projects to keep these young and enthusiastic minds well fed. It is important to note that, at this stage, the young adult is still seeking to situate themselves in society; to carve a niche for themselves; this directly results in the need to take on projects by which they feel they can contribute to society and add value to the lives of others. Therefore, there is massive interest among these youths in humanitarian and voluntary projects; charitable and social work.

Added to all this is the insane drive to see and experience the world; to learn and mix with other cultures; to be independent and to be open to possibilities. The drive to see the world does not, mind you, necessarily die out in later years; it is just generally more intense in early adulthood. It is a period that I have identified as the human's coming out; up to that point the young adult had been in the cocoon, developing and learning about how to face and deal with the world; up to that point, the young person must have been dying to get the chance to direct and control the direction their lives would take and up to that point, they would have envied adults the freedom they possessed.

First times are generally full of frenzy and, as to be expected, the young student loses no time in covering a number of trip to different places, taking in their fill of the differences in cultures, customs and people. They endeavour to get their hands 'dirty' with every new experience; for them this is the period to make all their mistakes and they do try to; they dabble into a variety of experiences addictive and inspiring; constructive and destructive; conservative and radical.

This phase has a lot in common with first years of a human's life when as a baby, the human would observe, investigate and go after every interesting thing sighted; this is the phase when babies are carefully watched and monitored as they are most prone to dangerous encounters at this time like playing with knives or hugging a hot electric iron; it is the same for the young adult, and, yet, phases like these should never be inhibited, never discouraged.

COUNT ME IN

A term that springs to mind to adequately denote the enthusiastic and daring invasion by youths into the world is youthful exuberance. It is not only an important period in the life of the young but also really important for society; if we did not have a vibrant youth body interested in the goings on of our world, then, in effect, the future of our institutions and establishments would be in jeopardy. Youthful exuberance is a much needed formation factor in the life of young people as they journey into the burdensome duty of being adults on whom the very structure of society rests.

The one vital area that youths are encouraged to take an active interest in is the political affairs of the State; there is not much need to explain why that is gravely relevant to and for the continued existence of the State. For some reason or another, the politics of the State is, inherently, another huge area of interest besieged by these budding minds. Naturally, I can only expect this sort of direction in passion from people willing to learn about their environment; the first place to always begin in such a quest is in knowing exactly how the laws and government of the society work. The huge interest generated by the political sector among young people is so much tied, I believe, to that undeniable need to be a part of something significant and the need to make their mark in society.

This drive is likely to have arisen naturally in the course of the evolution of the human; given the growth of the human community from simple to large and complex, it would have gradually become vital to individuals to express their individuality by some distinctive action, some action that would prove that they mattered and that they do have a role to play in society. On the other hand, symbiotically, this drive does provide the State with the necessary replacement to carry on in government and to ensure its continued survival; this is why universities and tertiary institutions are huge targets by various political units trying to win adherents and support.

Like all budding minds at any phase of development, the young adult is quite impressionable and a word well placed can so very easily fester into a deeply rooted belief and conviction not easily shaken, let alone removed. Alliances formed at this stage of a person's development have the tendency to carry on faithfully for a very long time through thick and thin. In very active universities, one can easily find the building blocks of practically every sector and units of the larger society from religious groups to trade unions; these groups would have identified that targeting and infusing their ideas into minds so open to new ideas and so keen to know can be a very big investment for the future. I have also found that the zeal with which these students attend to their chosen alliances and the attendant creeds is rarely surpassed. The idea that the youths are the strength and pillar of society does not just refer only to the physical side of things; ideas that run rampant in society are likely to be around for a lot longer if they are kept in the charge of the young.

This is a strategy that many ideological campaigns have employed to very good use. Sometimes, they have attended to, and begun with, people of younger ages than the young adults but the methods and results end up the same. This is a characteristic of human development that can be manipulated quite irresponsibly and such actions and their consequences, unfortunately, we have to live with.

HOW HIGH?

The utilisation of the raw and immense power and drive of youth is a well familiar occurrence; several civilisations have been raised and brought down in this way. Take the politics of Nationalism, for instance; it absolutely rests on the hope that a powerful enough human force can rise to back its, often destructive, policies. Human history is rippled with clear instances where the young have been practically used for politically selfish ends. And by, 'political' I refer to the root meaning of the word – a struggle for power, and not what we normally associate the word with in everyday parlance.

All forms of fundamentalism are directly aimed at this group of people and are, by the same token, fuelled by them actively, so that fundamentalist demonstrations would usually boil over into physical confrontation with people of opposing views. This is hardly surprising since youthful energy always requires a burnout route and very often that would have to be in some physical activity. Fundamentalist structures have always been raised and supported by institutions that have drunk and needed to retain power, from religious to governmental. The allegorical story of animal farm by Orwell suitably demonstrates the lethal effectiveness of youthful energy. In that story, Napoleon was 'smart' enough to raise and indoctrinate nine puppies who grew up to become his terror squad; to carry on with that story, I would imagine that Napoleon and his successors would set up a sort of 'training' institution for the puppies of those dogs or other dogs so they could serve the State in future.

In this state, the most confused is actually the youth who appears to be the most convinced about their beliefs. I am inclined to believe that the passionate adherence and fidelity that the young might show to a view point is born out of a deep need to be correct; a desire to be with the right folks; a dread of pledging their support, in their quest to make a difference, to the wrong idea. I did have a short spell in the Socialist party, more to have some understanding of its ideology; in that time, I attended a National convention of the party in London in the company of 'comrades' from my city and there, I noticed that there were people handing out fliers promoting the Communist party. Curiously, I asked a young university lad among us about this group and if their ideals would not be same with ours; he told me in no uncertain terms that they were not and ended his reply with 'we are the right group'.

This statement was in reference to, and making a distinction from, another ideology that would have a lot in common with Socialism yet the lad was very convinced and spelled it out that ours was the right group. How much more convinced and passionate would he be if he had to make a distinction from a totally opposed ideology? And, how equally convinced and passionate would the youths of the Communist party also be that they were in the right group? How convinced were the young crusaders of Christendom that they were in the right or the young Turks, that Jerusalem belonged to them; how convinced were the young martyrs of early Christianity; the young of Britain's imperial drive, the young of Nazi Germany; or fundamentalist young suicide bombers?

Every ideology with its own 'truth' is tempted to employ the weapon of youth to defend it and, in their insecurity of identity crisis, these youths are often happy to oblige. In itself, believing in a cause may not be a bad thing but getting totally and inextricably tied up with the cause, though, I find, very often is as it allows the individual no space with and in which to critically analyse and question the values upheld by the cause.

FOUNDATIONS ONCE DESTROYED

Ideology seems to stand out as one phenomenon of human society that can very easily lead to disastrous events and consequences. My first encounter and analysis with the notion of ideology was not a very comfortable one because I had to turn the spotlight on myself to pinpoint the various little 'ideologies' I had in safekeeping - none of these had anything to do with Santa Claus; I was in my twenties at the time. I think everyone has got an ideology; some sort of worked out principle trusted to provide direction and guidance through the confusion and mess that life can so often be. Looked at in this way, ideologies can be useful if in the random and chaos of our existence, we had the one constant thing to fall back on. It can, indeed, supply some sanity to our existence.

However, ideologies are, by their nature, very rigid and unmoving; they do not welcome criticisms and questions easily. There is a feeling of insecurity about them that tends to suggest that if one little iota of doubt is cast about them or if one small part of their tenet is shown to be flawed, the whole thing might fall apart. An ideology would generally impress upon the adherents to simply accept the principles and avoid debating them; some might stake the authenticity of their ideology on the very fact that it is not meant to be questioned, just believed; others are actually 'un-debatable' as there exists no real way of proving them true or false. And all ideologies are a passionate affair since they represent the one stable thing in the lives of the followers and the one standard by which they can place, not just their lives, but the world around them. Any confrontation of the ideology, therefore, is regarded as a confrontation of their very existence and this can be a very painful and sore experience.

It was this discomfort that I felt when I identified and reviewed certain ideologies that I adhered to. I do believe that this pain is very much foreseen and is very much associated to the very reason why ideologies will brook no debate. Ideologies promise a lot to people, offer them some sort of hope, comfort and stability, things, which are, often perceived as too good to be truly attainable but hoped for, anyway. Because this hope is a strong incentive, an ideology would, ordinarily regard as inconsequential, any shortfalls it may have within it on its march towards achieving its aim and providing the object of hope it has promised its faithful.

In the end, although faith in whatever principle might serve as a stable platform for people, the human mind cannot avoid its ever essential and naturally associated task of reviewing and analysing; flaws in ideologies will always be identified, and where they pose a threat to the well being of others, controlled and checked.

In my opinion, the problem lies in approaching the problem from the wrong end up; it is like building a skyscraper before investigating the structure of its foundations; if the structure were found faulty at a later date, the building would have to come down. It might help if views were developed upon analytical investigation so that the end result is not only open to criticisms since it was actually founded on them but it can always be improved by these criticisms. This would definitely provide a surer avenue to reaching a more realistic picture of the right course of action and the right way to go about it. Unfortunately, this sort of procedure does not offer the kind of dramatic and utopian hope or stability that an ideology can. Therefore, we can expect that ideologies will always thrive to satisfy that flip side of the human mind that would yearn for something deeper and better than what our ordinary existence can deliver.

TELL ME NO MORE

Some of the effects and consequences of ideological movements have been dire, plunging the world into bloodshed and chaos. Unchecked ideologies have very often fuelled the onset of periods of terror in every phase of human history. We know of some examples of these in history and we have the evidence of the terrorism that still grips the world today.

I do not suppose that there would be an altogether unanimous agreement that the terrorism we are currently battling with is the direct result of an ideological frenzy and I do not seek to make a case one way or another. What is certain, though, in the bitter bloody struggle the world is tied in, is that a great part of the Islamic world feels that they have been wronged, insulted and dominated by the West. As, with the first aims of the Ayatollah led revolution in the late seventies that longed to reclaim everything and every value purely Islamic, the interference of the West, directly or indirectly, in Islamic countries was certainly unwelcome. It was an interference of this kind, viewed as a desecration of Islam and Islamic structures that sparked the fight back by Bin Laden which culminated in a major tragedy for many people. However, many have also argued that even if the current spate of terrorist activities is not directly linked to an ideology, the barb of the perceived insult to Muslims would have sunk more deeply because of one.

Yet again, many would go ahead to debate the meaning of the term 'terrorist'; quite frequently, it has been qualified as a relative term. And often, and I do agree, one person's terrorist is another's freedom fighter. Nelson

Mandela was branded a terrorist at one time and later, proclaimed a freedom fighter by practically the same group of people. After all, there are some people in the world today who would judge Western structures as being terrorist, if only for the fact that by their actions, the world (recently) has seen a lot of violence and bloodshed; some might even propose that underneath the invasive actions of Britain and America might lie some ideology of superiority and the right to decide the fate of nations.

We are all too aware that either side justifying their actions and re-actions has brought several defences forward; however, I believe that there were several underlying and unshakable rules that must have been flouted to bring the world into its present mess. About the strongest attempt at a justification for the invasion of Iraq so far is that Iraq was really believed to have weapons of mass destruction and that, though, none were found, since Hussein had a poor human rights record, ignoring him might easily have led to the same results as ignoring Hitler did.

This defence does sound sentimentally strong – the war was in an effort to stop a tyrant and to prevent a possible genocide. However, I fear that if we throw aside the rationally sound basic principles for right and wrong judgement by justifying our actions with their intentions, we could be heading for an even greater disaster.

Those principles would find faulty the action of the overruling of the UN; find wrong, the invasion of a sovereign State without valid proof of its offence, which, even if found, would still not have given any individual country the unilateral right to invade another; and find reproachable the precedence this has set for any powerful enough nation to make war on another at will.

This does not, unfortunately, give any justification for terrorist actions (I do not see what can) that mastermind the death of innocent and uninvolved civilians because two wrongs do not make a right; besides, rational judgement will certainly not sanction any justification for an action that is simply misdirected; merely retaliatory – in that it is not directly defensive; and a blatant re-action – in that it is not an impulsive, involuntary and immediate response.

All we can expect this way is an unending cycle of bloodshed that will not, in any way, produce any winners but only show the principal actors in a world gone mad. Once again, though, I expect everyone knows this already.

COUNT ME OUT

The traumatic effects of terrorism and all other forms of conflict that arise from or that can be linked to one form of ideology or another have pushed a few people and governments to search for a middle ground answer. This middle ground would necessarily serve as a point of meeting for all the different factions in the society, along whatever lines; religious, ethnic, racial or even geographical. The first 'culprit', however, that people are all too happy to point out in the struggle against ideological movements is religion; a lot of people would hold that religion might so effectively be employed as the sharp barb in all forms of socio-ethnic divisions and tensions. This has led to the call for and the implementation, in some countries, of a secular State.

The secular State not only should not lend, at least in principle, any favour to any religious affiliation, it is expected to positively disfavour it in the public sector. Religion should be kept away from the education of the young in State schools; be barred from interfering with government laws and policies; have no place in the requirements of office and be given no recognition by the people in authority. France made this move not so long ago and their march towards secularisation was so intense that it was practically anti-religious.

It does strike me, though, that the only thing that can be worse than having one extreme is replacing it with another; religion has been shown to, evidently, be the life-blood of a great many people. Going positively anti-religious, therefore, might not be a good omen for the State in the long run. Suppressing the very essence of the existence of a good part of the citizenry can only spell an almost inevitable rise of societal tension. I do not believe also that religion is the only culprit when it comes to ideology and ideological movements. There are a myriad of ideologies that could, at any one time, be at work in the minds of groups of people ranging from racial to educational. Let us take the example of Scientism.

A lot of people who are, at present, pushing for a secular State in their countries are in favour of the rise and domination of Science, not only as a taught discipline but, practically, as an imbibed mindset; this is what might be referred to as Scientism – a secure belief that all our realistic, if not assured, answers can be found and should be laid in the pursuit of Science. Like every ideology, I expect it would brook no arguments and retains absoluteness in its 'truth'. But is it not quite exaggerating and over-estimating to maintain that Science provides all human answers? How wonderful would it have been for the human race if this were the case? The very nature of an ideology – which this view so readily demonstrates – makes out Scientism as a staunch refusal to identify weaknesses and flaws in its beliefs.

I actually believe that the State might benefit more if it were secular in government and in policies; it is the one avenue to reach full neutrality. However, the colourful differences that abound among people in ethnicity and religion should be welcomed and respected. Religious education should be a relatively private affair, so should all absolute and intolerant views of the world that some people might hold. I also recognise the importance of science being held up in schools as the only taught research discipline by which we can approach knowledge of our world, not because I think scientific truths are absolute, but because, after all, it is the only avenue open to the person devoid of any religious beliefs and should be employed, as well, to achieve neutrality in the education of people well and truly mixed.

DÉJÀ VU

It is almost certain that debates about the form that the Government should assume in its approach to faith and religion is not altogether new; very few issues in our world today do not have a preceding occurrence in the past from which we might draw lessons on how to tackle them. This is the whole purpose of history after all; to record events so that humans can always look back, see how far they have come and, so work out their future direction. This record is not only in print; it is much more in human experience. It is a little uncanny that very few events are quite original in human history; it is almost like someone, somewhere is bound to think of going down some route taken by another before, however discounted the experience has been, by history. Actually, it should not be surprising since we are basically the same – humans of all historical phases, especially from the moment we attained consciousness. The human mind might learn new lessons about wrong actions but the working of the mind is, in form, the same; our drives rarely change. They may vary according to the different situations we may find ourselves in and the different needs we might have at any point in time, but, in all the basic thrusts remain the same: power, fame, expansion, wealth, success, pleasure, community, knowledge, communion and family, to mention a few obvious ones.

The German philosopher Hegel talked about the spirit of human history and of the human race, past and present, being of one absolute spirit, and that that spirit is in constant rational progress. Others have put several variations of this view forward; they, generally, make out human history to be a single repetitive occurrence. Nietzsche, also German, elaborated on a theory of 'eternal occurrence' by which he postulated that everyone and all of history is really the continual repetition of the lives and actions of everyone in it. Well, I do not see any way in which these views may be tested, refuted or verified. However, we may, actually, not have enough to label this notion that there is a one-ness about human historical progress, complete drivel.

Often, popes have been required to apologise for offences of the Church ages before; Governments, for offences of their people in historical times; Nations for wrongs of their ancestors. Political leaders today would so often carry out an international action in direct relation to an event that may have happened many years before and people are always, continually being faced with the actions, and their consequences, of generations gone before them.

In all these cases, it is not simply a matter of remembering the past. Without orchestrating any performance, it does appear that past actions in human history are actually, at a sub-level, re-enacted for us in the present. Memorial ceremonies of the Second World War, of the Holocaust and of various genocides in various countries are practically as physically and emotionally significant for people in every age and time as the real events were. This phenomenon might actually denote the inherent oneness of spirit that all human history shares, rather like one living undying entity with a growing soul, if I am still making sense.

I would like to think that this quality is directly a result of the 'spiritual' nature of not just human life but also human actions. The popular adage 'the evils that men do live after them' is but a little pointer to the undying continuity that the human 'spirit' (consciousness) can generate, so real, that it is, practically, physically inherited by the people of future generations. This theory might not, in itself, be anywhere near original; if I think it, it is quite possible that others have too; if Hegel thought along those lines, there is no telling the millions before him who might have as well. Or how else, do you think, has been sprung the belief and theory of re-incarnation?

DEFINITELY MY MESS

Human history must have taught us, no doubt, about the various attempts by humans to structure the running of their society along fair and equitable lines. These attempts have not always gone according to plan, especially, when the leaders had to accommodate their individual yearning for power and fame. Some governmental structures have been established, therefore, time and time again to favour a few against the majority. These few people were the special, elite, noble, chosen and ruling class among and around whom the power of running the State seemed to revolve. Aristocracy may have had its good points but the ill-treatment it is bound to have accorded the masses that could have no say in the actions and direction of government, would have made it a wrong option for human societies.

Aristocracy may have and, generally, was the direct offshoot of another form of government that depended on religious laws as the laws of society. Theocracy required that the people not only had the one religion but that the religion was, in effect, the State. The function of the leaders was only to see to it that these laws were kept and offenders punished. Apparently, over time especially, in the Renaissance and, subsequently, the Modernist era, the human society tossed aside every form of religious and theocratic domination that stifled their freedom in determining own affairs.

Human history, then, went through interesting forms of government that were altogether dissatisfying, some of which were forms of Autocracy, Oligarchy and

Monarchy. In time, many societies settled for Democracy – the government determined and controlled by the people.

In simple terms, Democracy is the government of the majority, which is often used to denote the overall will of the people. In the same vein, however, this characteristic of democracy is seen to marginalise the views of the minority, who, though, may boast a smaller number of people have every right to equal treatment as every other person or group. Perhaps, when studied closely, we might find that no system of government, much like every human undertaking, can be perfect and that Democracy seems to offer the best possible arrangement to give to the people the desires of the people.

Others may disagree; Democracy has been seen not only to marginalise sections of society but, by employing its free economic arm of capitalism [does present day Democracies], to push people farther into poverty and widen the gap that already exists between the haves and the have-nots. Democracy, or what it is termed to be in today's world, is only a disguised attempt to give free rein to the owners of the factors of production to accumulate more wealth at the expense of human labour.

My one question is framed rather like the chicken and egg question; how did these wealthy entrepreneurs become what they are? Does that offer some hope that with Democracy and Capitalism, anyone too has the chance to become equally successful? A simple answer to this might be the cynical suggestion that, going with dedicated toil, good business acumen and, of course, an education alone, one average person in ten thousand might get to that 'success' in, say, just fifty years. This may not actually sound as terribly depressing as we might have expected, especially, when we think that, at least, there is the slight promise of a chance, a possibility. However, this statistic does not entirely reflect any true equality in society.

It is at this juncture that the arch-enemy of Capitalism – Communism – rears its head; Communism would promise everything that Capitalism does not seem able to give, namely, the joy of a classless society where the wealth of the nation belongs to all and is equitably distributed among all along fair lines of their needs and their (labour) input. However, with theories like that the establishment of Communism requires a class conflict and a revolution before it can be successfully implemented, it is not hard to explain the attendant violence and suppression of people that have been found in Communist regimes.

COMRADES' HAVEN

If Communism promises a classless society, then, by that very fact, it would not recognise the individual or individual rights. This is a direct infringement on the essence of a person – freedom – and, naturally, would, inevitably, spark off some resistance at some level and at some point. And, of course, this resistance would have to be seen to if Communism were to have any chance of working within the State. However, since it is in the nature of Communism to not recognise the individual, no compromise can really be achieved; the only way out would be through the use of force. It would seem, therefore, that Communism is not a workable system, if the inalienable rights of individuals are to be taken seriously.

Over time, however, there has been the wide promotion of the larger theory of Socialism, of which Communism is a branch. As a response to the shortfalls of Communism, Socialism does not promise an entirely classless society but that factors of production and the distribution of wealth remain under the control of the public. Socialism would push for the nationalization of main key industries and for some State regulation over the market. Modern Socialism does not also stand in opposition to Democracy; Socialists envisage a framework where the public democratically retain ownership of a large portion of the property of the State and for a limited, not cut out, private property ownership.

On the surface of it, this does sound like the perfect solution to the problem of government and the fairest answer to economic problems. It would take a little analysis, however, of the various governments who, at least claim to, practice Socialism to understand why it may not be completely perfect.

It is widely understood that market competition, instigated by private ownership of property, is a big factor in the growth of economies, which will at some point benefit the people. I have experienced various economies where the public sector is so appallingly deficient due to poor management that the people are actually crying out for the privatization of government industries. The notion that everybody's problem is nobody's problem can so hold true in a setting where the public hold absolute sway over the property of the nation.

Since the drive to make profit can be assured to galvanize private entrepreneurs into bringing about organization and efficiency in their industries, privatization does have the main ingredients for better public service. It is true, on the other hand, that these entrepreneurs can easily manipulate their labour force and that privatization can be a direct threat to employment as the jobs of workers are never really secure with private companies. Indeed, not many would find it plausible that key government structures are given over to private management; that could spell disaster for the people. One thing, though, it might help to place no bar on private ownership and the expansion drive of individuals; it is their right if they have worked hard for it.

The government has a responsibility to protect the welfare of the people by retaining control over major public structures directly connected to the wellbeing of the people and the growth of the economy such as health, education, communication and transport while allowing direct competition from private groups; that way, it might ensure that the ills of monopoly are prevented both in the public and private sector.

It has never seemed that we are very much closer to perfection in any absolute system of government than when we first started out. None seem to have provided the full answer for any human society and various governments might have found that, quite often, a hybrid of systems is needed to effect economic growth. Are the current capitalist structures of some rather successful countries today not based on the direct involvement of the public ownership of State property in direct competition with privately run businesses on which there are very little limits placed on expansion but plenty of government monitoring? I think so.

POSTSCRIPT

The journey of humankind might have been filled with the spectacle of eventful repetitive cycles, most concentrically contained one within another; and even in orbits are these cycles made directly manifest to effect the seasonal variations we experience. However the cycle of our very existence is manifestly demonstrated within and around us. The throb of the environment as a living organism defines in its cyclical path the pattern in Nature. Structure may pile on structure but to the dust does the call terminate, which is in itself the origin of structure, albeit indirectly.

Our actions, though, may defy structure, totally bound in freedom; the freedom of choice tethered to the responsibility for right and by that same token might we be said to be determined by Nature to act our role and situate with meaning all that she has spawned. By our freedom, we may choose to veer from the course but often have we found that on that same course is to be found any true direction away from the ills of our actions and the consequences of our choices. By rational knowledge, we may have inherited the privileged status of human and embodied that role by explorations, exercising our mental abilities but our task is ever ongoing as all of Nature demands.

If Nature were to speak in our language and to us her message impart; if we do pay attention in an attempt to understand, our knowledge would still not be conclusive nor our search ended because we would have realised, in her drift, much like the laughter of the gods, the infinity of wonder, the wonder of space, the passage of time, the flux of change, the uncertainty of principles, the rigidity of laws, the swell of chance, the roll of dice, the laughter of the gods, the shadow of death, the limits of understanding, the light of consciousness, the pain of effort, the sweat of labour, the company of community, the union of communion, the result of addition, the absurdity of numbers, the dilemma of morality, the weight of guilt, the beauty of meaning, the totality of value, the profusion of emotion, the payment for sentiment, the joy of liberty, the power of ideas, the depth of belief, the fear of terror, the hurt of bloodshed, the crush of suicide, the finality of death, the emptiness of non-being and the lessons of history, the spirit of humanity.

Printed in the United States
122509LV00001B/131/A